International

Labour and Employment Compliance in the United Arab Emirates

Ninth Edition

Sara Khoja

Sarit Thomas

This publication is part of the International Labour and Employment Compliance Handbook, available on www.kluwerlawonline.com

Editors: Salvador del Rey and Robert J. Mignin
Associate Editor: Juan Bonilla

INTERNATIONAL BAR ASSOCIATION

the global voice of
the legal profession

Wolters Kluwer

Published by:
Kluwer Law International B.V.
PO Box 316
2400 AH Alphen aan den Rijn
The Netherlands
E-mail: lrs-sales@wolterskluwer.com
Website: www.wolterskluwer.com/en/solutions/kluwerlawinternational

Sold and distributed by:
Wolters Kluwer Legal & Regulatory U.S.
7201 McKinney Circle
Frederick, MD 21704
United States of America
E-mail: customer.service@wolterskluwer.com

ISBN 978-94-035-4444-1

e-Book: ISBN 978-94-035-4465-6
web-PDF: ISBN 978-94-035-4475-5

All listed titles are also available on lrus.wolterskluwer.com

1. Argentina: Julio César Stefanoni Zani & Enrique Alfredo Betemps, *Labour and Employment Compliance in Argentina, 10th edition*, 2022 (ISBN 978-94-035-4332-1)
2. Australia: John Tuck, Stephen Price, Rosemary Roach, Jack de Flamingh, Nicholas Ellery & Nick Le Mare, *Labour and Employment Compliance in Australia, 6th edition*, 2021 (ISBN 978-94-035-3914-0)
3. Belgium: Chris Van Olmen, *Labour and Employment Compliance in Belgium, 7th edition*, 2022 (ISBN 978-94-035-4374-1)
4. Brazil: Rodrigo Seizo Takano, Andrea Giamondo Massei & Murilo Caldeira Germiniani, *Labour and Employment Compliance in Brazil, 9th edition*, 2022 (ISBN 978-94-035-4991-0)
5. Canada: Kevin Coon & Adrian Ishak, *Labour and Employment Compliance in Canada, 2nd edition*, 2014 (ISBN 978-90-411-5637-2)
6. Chile: Gerardo Otero A., María Dolores Echeverría F., María de los Ángeles Fernández S. & Javier Sabido, *Labour and Employment Compliance in Chile, 10th edition*, 2022 (ISBN 978-94-035-4404-5)
7. China: King & Wood Mallesons, *Labour and Employment Compliance in China, 6th edition*, 2021 (ISBN 978-94-035-3894-5)
8. France: Pascale Lagesse, *Labour and Employment Compliance in France, 10th edition*, 2022 (ISBN 978-94-035-4384-0)
9. Germany: Gerlind Wisskirchen & Martin Lützeler, *Labour and Employment Compliance in Germany, 10th edition*, 2022 (ISBN 978-94-035-4454-0)
10. India: Manishi Pathak, *Labour and Employment Compliance in India, 10th edition*, 2022 (ISBN 978-94-035-4362-8)
11. Ireland: Duncan Inverarity & Ailbhe Dennehy, *Labour and Employment Compliance in Ireland, 8th edition*, 2021 (ISBN 978-94-035-3911-9)
12. Israel: Pnina Broder-Manor, Helen Raziel & Ilan Winder, *Labour and Employment Compliance in Israel, 9th edition*, 2022 (ISBN 978-94-035-4424-3)
13. Italy: Angelo Zambelli, *Labour and Employment Compliance in Italy, 10th edition*, 2022 (ISBN 978-94-035-4372-7)
14. Japan: Yoshikazu Sugino, *Labour and Employment Compliance in Japan, 10th edition*, 2022 (ISBN 978-94-035-4342-0)
15. Republic of Korea: Sang Wook Cho, Soojung Lee & Christopher Mandel, *Labour and Employment Compliance in the Republic of Korea, 8th edition*, 2022 (ISBN 978-94-035-4434-2)
16. Mexico: Oscar De La Vega Gómez, *Labour and Employment Compliance in Mexico, 10th edition*, 2022 (ISBN 978-94-035-4414-4)
17. The Netherlands: Els de Wind & Cara Pronk, *Labour and Employment Compliance in the Netherlands, 5th edition*, 2022 (ISBN 978-94-035-1594-6)
18. Poland: Barbara Jóźwik, *Labour and Employment Compliance in Poland, 9th edition*, 2021 (ISBN 978-94-035-3675-0)
19. Russia: Anna-Stefaniya Chepik, *Labour and Employment Compliance in Russia*, 2013 (ISBN 978-90-411-4925-1)

20. Saudi Arabia: Sara Khoja & Sarit Thomas, *Labour and Employment Compliance in Saudi Arabia, 5th edition*, 2022 (ISBN 978-94-035-4394-9)
21. South Africa: Susan Stelzner, Stuart Harrison, Brian Patterson & Zahida Ebrahim, *Labour and Employment Compliance in South Africa, 10th edition*, 2022 (ISBN 978-94-035-4474-8)
22. Spain: Salvador del Rey, Ana Campos & Sergi Gálvez Duran, *Labour and Employment Compliance in Spain, 10th edition*, 2022 (978-94-035-4352-9)
23. Turkey: Sertaç Kökenek & Elif Nur Çakır Vurgun, *Labour and Employment Compliance in Turkey, 7th edition*, 2021 (ISBN 978-94-035-3901-0)
24. United Arab Emirates: Sara Khoja & Sarit Thomas, *Labour and Employment Compliance in the United Arab Emirates, 9th edition*, 2022 (ISBN 978-94-035-4444-1)
25. United Kingdom: Ed Mills, Ailie Murray, Anna West, Gareth Walls, Emmie Ellison & Elliot English, *Labour and Employment Compliance in The United Kingdom, 3rd edition*, 2022 (ISBN 978-94-035-4464-9)
26. United States: Andrew J. Boling, Amy de La Lama, William Dugan, Chris Guldberg, Brian Hengesbaugh, Robert J. Mignin, Virginia Mohr, John M. Murphy & Ginger Partee, *Labour and Employment Compliance in the United States, 7th edition*, 2022 (ISBN 978-94-035-3921-8)

International Bar Association
The Global Voice of the Legal Profession

The International Bar Association (IBA), established in 1947, is the world's leading organization of international legal practitioners, bar associations and law societies. The IBA influences the development of international law reform and shapes the future of the legal profession throughout the world. It has a membership of over 40,000 individual lawyers and almost 200 bar associations and law societies spanning all continents. It has considerable expertise in providing assistance to the global legal community.

Grouped into two divisions – the Legal Practice Division and the Public and Professional Interest Division – the IBA covers all practice areas and professional interests, providing members with access to leading experts and up-to-date information. Through the various committees of the divisions, the IBA enables an interchange of information and views among its members as to laws, practices and professional responsibilities relating to the practice of business law around the globe. Additionally, the IBA's high-quality publications and world-class conferences provide unrivalled professional development and network-building opportunities for international legal practitioners and professional associates.

The IBA's Bar Issues Commission provides an invaluable forum for IBA member organisations to discuss all matters relating to law at an international level.

The IBA's Human Rights Institute (IBAHRI) works across the Association, to promote, protect and enforce human rights under a just rule of law, and to preserve the independence of the judiciary and the legal profession worldwide.

Other institutions established by the IBA include the Southern Africa Litigation Centre and the International Legal Assistance Consortium.

Employment and Industrial Relations Law Committee

The aims of the committee are to develop and exchange knowledge of employment and industrial relations law and practice. Members support each other through the provision of innovative ideas and practical assistance on day-to-day issues. In addition, through its journal and through presentations, conferences, the committee ensures the dissemination of up-to-date law and practice in this highly important business area.

International Bar Association Global Employment Institute

The IBA Global Employment Institute (IBA GEI) was formed in early 2010 for the purpose of developing for multinationals and worldwide institutions a global and strategic approach to the key legal issues in the human resources and human capital fields.

Drawing on the resources and expertise of the IBA membership, the IBA GEI will provide a unique contribution in the field of employment, discrimination and immigration law, on a diverse range of global issues, to private and public organizations throughout the world. The IBA GEI is designed to enhance the management, performance and productivity of these organizations and help achieve best practice in their human capital and management functions from a strategic perspective.

The IBA GEI will become the leading voice and authority on global HR issues by virtue of having a number of the world's leading labour and employment practitioners in its ranks, and the support and resource of the world's largest association of international lawyers.

Further information

International Bar Association, 4th Floor, 10 St Bride Street, London EC4A 4AD, United Kingdom, Tel: +44 (0)20 7842 0090, Fax: +44 (0)20 7842 0091, E-mail: member@int-bar.org, www.ibanet.org

About the International Labour and Employment Compliance Handbook

From 1976 through 1988, the International Bar Association and Kluwer Law International published the groundbreaking International Handbook on Contracts of Employment. This Handbook provided one of the first global overviews of the law of the international employment relationship.

Since publishing the first edition, globalization of business has created an increased demand for knowledge of labor and employment laws throughout the world. Therefore, along with Kluwer, we decided to publish an updated Handbook which we have titled the International Labour and Employment Compliance Handbook.

This new Handbook was intended to be a practical guide by providing a general overview of key labor and employment issues in multiple jurisdictions. Each chapter was written so that it is easy to understand by lawyers and non-lawyers alike. Each country author has also followed a standard outline to assist readers in analysing employment issues in each country.

The first edition of this new Handbook included nineteen (19) different countries.

This Handbook would not have been possible without the help and assistance of many people. Most importantly, the individual country authors are all distinguished legal practitioners who spent considerable time drafting and revising their country reports to meet difficult deadlines. We thank each of them. Our friends at Kluwer, especially Ewa Szkatula, have done a wonderful job in keeping the editors and the authors on schedule. Finally, we want to also express our gratitude to Cuatrecasas, Gonçalves Pereira, and Baker & McKenzie LLP for their valuable assistance in the coordination and organization of this project. Our warmest thanks to each of them.

Because of the success of the Handbook, Wolters Kluwer Law & Business decided to publish each country report also as a separate book to give a choice in obtaining the information. We hope this new format will be a helpful and useful resource just like the Handbook. Both formats are available in print and online.

The Editors

Salvador del Rey Guanter
Robert J. Mignin

March 2013

Table of Contents

United Arab Emirates

AUTHORS

Sara Khoja

Sara Khoja specializes in employment law, advising corporate clients in a variety of sectors, including oil and gas, construction, hospitality, retail, technology, shipping and insurance. She qualified in England and Wales in 2002.

She is a partner in the employment practice for Clyde and Co LLP's Middle Eastern and African Offices in the United Arab Emirates (UAE), the State of Qatar, the Kingdom of Saudi Arabia and the Sultanate of Oman. Clyde and Co LLP is the largest international law firm in the Arabian Gulf region and has had a presence in the region for over thirty years. Sara is based in Clyde and Co's Dubai office, having joined in 2008 when the practice was established, where she provides employment advice for the Middle East region, and in particular, the Arabian Gulf Cooperation Council Member States. Sara provides advice on all aspects of employment law, including recruitment, termination, terms and conditions of employment (benefits, bonuses and remuneration), and the application of quotas for the employment of nationals in various Arabian Gulf countries.

Sara also has a particular focus on multi-jurisdictional projects and issues arising out of employee mobilization, including the territorial reach of UK employment law.

She regularly presents at seminars and workshops as part of Clyde and Co's regular client programme and at external events organized by various business councils and HR consultancy firms. She has written for a number of publications, including the *New Law Journal*, *Asian Counsel*, *Solicitors*

Journal and *Personnel Today*. She is also regularly quoted in publications such as *Gulf News*, *Gulf Business*, and *Emirates 24/7*.

ADDRESS

Sara Khoja,
Partner,
Employment Group,
Clyde & Co LLP,
Dubai Office: PO Box 7001, Level 15, Rolex Tower, Sheikh Zayed Road,
Dubai, United Arab Emirates,
Tel.: + 971 50 552 9961
Fax: +971 4 384 4004
E-mail: Sara.Khoja@clydeco.ae

Sarit Thomas

Sarit is a Professional Support Lawyer within the Clyde & Co LLP knowledge-management team based in the firm's Dubai office, within the employment department. Sarit is admitted to practise as a solicitor in England and Wales and has been based in the Middle East region since 2008.

Sarit's role includes the creation of precedent documentation, researching and advising on recent developments in employment law and keeping the employment team's knowledge and skills up-to-date. As part of her role, Sarit organizes, prepares and delivers training both internally to the firm and externally at client seminars, as well as managing the team's internal training programme. Sarit also prepares and delivers training programmes with the Dubai Legal Affairs Department to registered lawyers in Dubai. Sarit writes legal articles and contributes to the team's client bulletins, as well as to a number of external legal publications, and is responsible for managing the team's know-how and template database.

ADDRESS

Sarit Thomas,
Professional Support Lawyer,
Clyde & Co LLP,
Dubai Office: PO Box 7001, Level 15, Rolex Tower, Sheikh Zayed Road,
Dubai, United Arab Emirates,
Tel.: + 971 56 548 8158
Fax: +971 4 384 4004
E-mail: Sarit.Thomas@clydeco.ae

Legal Compliance in United Arab Emirates

1. LEGAL FRAMEWORK: EMPLOYMENT LAWS IN UNITED ARAB EMIRATES

The main legislation that applies to all businesses operating in the United Arab Emirates (UAE) with respect to employment matters is UAE Law No. 33 of 2021 regulating labour relations (the 'Labour Law'), Cabinet Resolution No. 1 of 2022, on the executive regulations of the Labour Law ('Executive Regulations') and where applicable Ministerial Resolutions issued by the Ministry of Human Resources and Emiratisation (MHRE). Federal Decree No. 47 of 2021 on the uniform general rules of work in the UAE was also published in the same edition of the gazette as the new Labour Law. This decree seeks to align the public sector and the private sector on a number of employment entitlements by setting out rules which apply across both sectors.

The Labour Law came into effect on 2 February 2022 repealing the previous federal labour law (Law No. 8 of 1980). The Labour Law is a federal law and applies to each Emirate within the UAE and, with a few minor exceptions, covers all UAE employees in the private sector. Thus, its application is mandatory for all individuals carrying out work in the UAE. Other laws of note in the labour field are the UAE Immigration Law, UAE Crimes and Penalties Law, the UAE Civil Code, Commercial Code and the UAE Data Protection Law.

Some of the free trade zones in the UAE have their own employment regulations, but with the exception of the Dubai International Financial Centre (DIFC) and the Abu Dhabi Global Market (ADGM), ultimately all employees, whether employed by a business operating within a free zone or 'onshore' in the UAE, are subject to the Labour Law. Within the ADGM, employment matters are governed by ADGM Employment Regulations

2019 (ADGM Employment Regulations), and within the DIFC, employment matters are governed by DIFC Law No. 2 of 2019, as amended.

Similar to other labour laws, any provision in an agreement to waive any right or requirement granted by the Labour Law, the DIFC Employment Law or the ADGM Employment Regulations has no effect, except where expressly permitted under the Labour Law, the DIFC Employment Law or the ADGM Employment Regulations, as applicable. The requirements of each law are considered minimum requirements. Furthermore, any terms and conditions of employment in any agreement that are more favourable to an employee shall be valid.

The public sector has its own employment law setting out public-sector staff grades, promotion tracks, and remuneration and benefits packages. This legislation is beyond the scope of this chapter and would not be applicable to private-sector employees, even where they are working for the public-sector authorities under service contracts or agreements.

Government-owned entities (many established by decree) employ a large number of employees, and the status of such employees is often unclear. If established by decree, the decree will often provide for the employees of the entity to be covered by the civil service law or for employee matters to be regulated by the entity's own employment regulations once issued. In the absence of such provisions, employees of such entities are subject to the Labour Law. There has also been an increasing trend in the Labour Courts in the past five years to apply the Labour Law to these entities in a desire to regulate their employment practices and give employees access to the Labour Courts and to a minimum floor of entitlements.

The Labour Law is administered and enforced by the UAE MHRE. The MHRE issues regular ministerial decisions and administrative circulars for the execution of the Labour Law, and that are supplementary to it. Often, these resolutions and decrees are authorized by Cabinet Resolutions which permit a quicker mechanism for introducing legislative innovation, rather than the passing of new federal laws. All employers (apart from government-owned entities, free zone companies and specifically exempt employers in certain sectors) are required to register with the MHRE.

The DIFC Employment Law is administered and enforced by the DIFC Authority, and the ADGM Employment Regulations are administered by the Board of Directors of the ADGM.

The remaining free trade zones each have their own free zone authority, which administers and enforces that free zone's employment regulations and the Labour Law.

Certain sectors will also be regulated by other government authorities; for example, teachers will also come under the jurisdiction of the Ministry of Education, those employed in hotels and above will come under the jurisdiction of the Ministry of Economy and the local municipality, and pilots must comply with regulations issued by the Civil Aviation Authority, banks fall under the UAE Central Bank's regulation, and insurance companies will fall under the jurisdiction of the Insurance Authority. Care needs to be exercised with regard to other regulations or by-laws for specific sectors issued other than by the MHRE.

2. CONTRACTS OF EMPLOYMENT

2.1. OVERVIEW

Under the Labour Law, employment contracts may be written or oral, and an employee may use all means of evidence available to him or her to determine the terms and conditions of the employment contract. However, without a written employment contract, it is practically extremely difficult for an employee to establish his status and also his entitlements and thereby enforce them. In the interests of clarity and to protect employees, the MHRE (and free zone authorities) requires each employee to have an employment contract and an offer letter registered with it. Under the Labour Law, all documents are required to be issued in Arabic. However, apart from documents submitted and registered with government authorities, it is a commonplace for documents to be issued in English.

2.2. WRITTEN EMPLOYMENT CONTRACTS

An expatriate employee seeking to live and work 'onshore' (i.e., outside a free zone) in the UAE must in the first instance sign an offer letter, in a form prescribed by the MHRE (the 'Offer Letter') and thereafter an employment contract, in English and Arabic, in a form prescribed by the MHRE ('MHRE Contract') which must reflect the terms of the Offer Letter unless the proposed alterations are to the employee's advantage and are accepted by the employee and the MHRE. The Offer Letter and the MHRE Contract are an integral part of the sponsorship application process for a UAE work permit and residency visa. Such documents must be entered into and registered with the MHRE before it will issue a labour card for the employee. The Labour Law requires contracts to be in writing and for two copies to be executed, one for the employer and one for the employee, and for a fixed term of up to three years. Employers have twelve months from 2 February 2022 to convert all their unlimited term contracts to fixed-term contracts with a maximum term of three years. Under the previous labour law, two types of employment contracts were in place, fixed-term contracts and unlimited-term contract. Fixed-term contracts start on one date and end on another and they did not provide for the ability to terminate on notice. Under the new Labour Law only a fixed-term contract may be issued up to a term not exceeding three years, which may be terminated early on notice.

Employers will often have a more comprehensive, supplementary contract of employment, which will be construed against the employer and, therefore, will be enforceable only to the extent that it confers additional benefits on the employee and does not contradict the Labour Law and other laws of the UAE. Employees who are UAE nationals or nationals of a Gulf Cooperation Council (GCC) Member State will also have an MHRE Contract, with slightly different provisions. Free zone authorities may have their own template of prescribed form employment contract which must be registered with the authority for each employee. However the majority of free zone authorities will permit an employer to register its own template contract, but practice in this regard varies widely.

The only information required by the Labour Law and Executive Regulations to be specified in an employment contract are the following:

- Name and address of the employer.
- Name, nationality and date of birth of employee.
- Proof of employee identity.
- Employee qualifications.
- Job or occupation details.
- Commencement date.
- Place of work.
- Working hours.
- Rest days.
- Probationary period, if any.
- Contract term.
- Salary, including benefits and allowances.
- Annual leave entitlements.
- Notice period.
- Procedures for terminating the employment contract.

The maximum probationary period is six months, which may be applied only once during employment. An employee's contract can be terminated on fourteen days' written notice during this period. If an employee wishes to resign during this period and move to a new UAE employer, thirty days' notice must be served, and the new employer is obliged to compensate the current employer for the recruitment costs incurred.

Requirement for the new employer to compensate the current employer also applies where the employee resigns during the probation period, exits the UAE and then returns within a period of three months. The DIFC Employment Law provides for a maximum period of six months' probationary period which must be specified in the contract. During this period, either party may terminate the contract of employment immediately without cause. The ADGM Employment Regulations provide for a maximum probationary period of six months. During this period either party may terminate the contract without cause on one week's notice (or without notice if the termination is 'for cause').

In the DIFC and ADGM, there is no prescribed form of employment contract that is required to be lodged with the relevant free zone authority. There is, however, a requirement that all employees (unless they are only to be employed for one month or less) receive written employment contracts that are at least compliant with the minimum legal provisions: under which an employee is entitled to receive a contract setting out the name of employer, job title, date that the employment started, place of work, duration of contract if fixed, entitlements to leave, salary and benefits (rates and payment dates), hours of work, notice, and disciplinary and grievance procedure details. The DIFC Authority may request sight of any written contract for a particular employee and in recent years has adopted a practice of requiring a copy of the signed contract to be submitted when an employee is first recruited and registered with the Authority.

2.3. ORAL CONTRACTS

Oral contracts are recognized under the Labour Law and the Civil Code and may arise from the conduct of the parties, oral communications and express agreement. However, as explained above in practice, due to regulatory requirements, it should be a rare occasion where an employment relationship arises, which is not evidenced by a written employment contract.

2.4. EMPLOYEE HANDBOOKS

Employee Handbooks are not compulsory in the UAE. However, every employer will need to have the following workplace policies issued in writing: a list of work instructions, disciplinary penalties, promotions, bonuses, a Disciplinary Policy and a Health and Safety Policy.

In practice, the use of Employee Handbooks is commonplace, and many multinational employers will operate globally integrated Employee Handbooks. An employer issuing such a Handbook, and written policies in general, needs to exercise care as to whether such policies become part of an employee's terms and conditions of employment, either expressly or through custom and practice. Such considerations are particularly important with respect to policies such as a redundancy policy, benefits policy or termination procedure policy. Where policies are issued in writing, are widely known by employees and relied upon, there will be a strong argument that such policies have become part of the employee's terms and conditions of employment. The DIFC Employment Law and ADGM Employment Regulations expressly require an employer to specify in the contract what provisions are subject to company policy, and which are contractual, or not, and can be therefore varied on written notice.

2.5.   JOB DESCRIPTIONS

While job descriptions are not mandatory, the job title is required to be specified in the employment contract. However, such documents are commonly issued in the UAE, depending on the employer's custom and practice. Where a job description is issued, an employer could experience difficulty in changing the employee's role or the scope of the role without the employee's consent. Job titles can be a contentious issue within the UAE immigration and work authorization framework. The MHRE and the Department of Immigration have a list of approximately forty prescribed job titles and will expect a candidate's educational qualifications to match the job title. Where there is no correlation, the job title request will be rejected. The MHRE will also expect any individual to be described as a manager to have a four-year degree in a subject correlating to the title requested.

2.6.   OFFER LETTERS

It is mandatory to issue the prescribed form of MHRE Offer Letter in the UAE where the employer falls under the jurisdiction of the MHRE.

2.7.   CHECKLIST OF DO'S AND DON'TS

– Ensure that the MHRE prescribed form of Offer Letter and Contract is issued.
– Ensure any supplementary contract issued is clear and consistent.
– Ensure that all documents issued to an employee are consistent with the terms of the MHRE Contract (or free zone contract equivalent) and documents submitted to UAE authorities.
– Consider whether any Employee Handbook should be contractual.

3. RECRUITING, INTERVIEWING, SCREENING AND HIRING EMPLOYEES

3.1. OVERVIEW

The Labour Law does not set out any procedures or guidance on recruitment, such as a duty to advertise in certain publications or apply a particular interview or recruitment process.

In practice, it is the MHRE that will monitor recruitment and in particular the employment of UAE nationals. The MHRE is under a duty not to approve a work permit application unless the individual has professional competencies or educational qualifications that the UAE needs, and provided its records show that, among the UAE nationals registered within its employment section, there are no unemployed nationals capable of performing the work. It has been known for a work permit application to be rejected on the basis that there are registered unemployed UAE nationals capable of undertaking the role.

The UAE economy has historically been dominated by the oil industry, and the emphasis has been on public-sector employment with nearly 90% of the UAE national workforce being employed in the public sector. However, with a relatively young population (more than half of which is under the age of 25), the private sector (made up increasingly of foreign investors and companies) is being looked to for job creation, and a number of measures are being introduced to encourage, and in some cases compel, private-sector employers to employ UAE nationals. Such a policy is generally known as 'Emiratisation'.

The MHRE has over the last number of years launched a series of various Emiratisation programmes seeking to increase UAE national participation within the private sector (none of which have affected companies within the free zones). The 'Tawteen' (meaning Emiratisation) programme was launched on 7 December 2016 in an effort to promote and facilitate Emiratisation in the private sector. Employers were selected to enrol in the Tawteen scheme and receive privileges and benefits that would otherwise not be available once they hit certain Emiratisation targets and are prepared to train and invest in Emirati nationals.

There were four elements to the Tawteen programme, namely (i) communication strategy and labour market policies where the programme sought to motivate and engage Emirati nationals to work in the private sector; (ii) MHRE support given to companies recruiting through the Tawteen portal and to Emirati jobseekers; (iii) Emirati jobseekers guidance, learning and development opportunities; and (iv) Tawteen partners where companies could apply to join the Tawteen Partners' Club, subject to meeting certain criteria, and take advantage of various privileges.

Companies which were caught by the programme were required to post new vacancies through the Tawteen online portal known as Tawteen Gate to allow Emirati nationals a right of first refusal on job opportunities. Employers were required to demonstrate that they have considered and interviewed registered UAE nationals but not been able to find the right candidate in order to then apply through the online immigration portal to sponsor a foreign national for work and residency purposes.

A new system of labour market testing was introduced in 2019 targeting mainland private-sector companies applying for new work permits for designated professions in skill levels 1–3. Employers seeking to hire new employees were required to attend an MHRE open day (as advised by MHRE) and interview UAE nationals who had been selected by the MHRE, and in instances where the employer did not wish to consider the selected candidates further, the employer was required to justify their reasons. Whether or not an employer was subject to labour market testing was dependant on the role being advertised, the level of education required for the role and the number of employees the employer employs.

In September 2018 MHRE rolled out labour awareness training requiring new and renewed employment permit applicants in select professions and designations to attend an awareness session before their employment contract is approved by the MHRE as part of the labour permit application.

The MHRE introduced a new scheme called 'Nafis' which came into effect on 13 September 2021. The scheme aims to bridge the gap between the private and public sectors and create 75,000 new jobs in the private sector for UAE nationals. As part of the scheme there are eleven different initiatives, including government subsidies to employers, training schemes, pension support and many others. The scheme aims to increase Emiratisation rates in the private sector by a minimum of 2% annually for skilled occupations within companies with more than fifty employees, with the aim of reaching 10% by 2026. While the scheme is not yet obligatory, new legislation mandating an increase in quotas is expected.

The MHRE's role is supplemented by the National Human Resource Development and Employment Authority (commonly known as 'TANMIA'), which is a federal government independent authority whose aim is to create job opportunities for the UAE national workforce, enhance the skills and productivity of the national workforce, and recommend relevant policies to the UAE government.

A series of Ministerial Decisions (No. 10 of 1998, No. 42 of 2005, No. 43 of 2005) introduced specific quotas for UAE nationals' employment on a sector basis: 4% in banking, 5% in insurance and 2% in trade sector firms (with the percentage required to rise year on year). New minimum quotas are expected to be issued in line with the increased Emiratisation targets set out above. A business not meeting these targets is subject to higher administrative fees from the MHRE and the Immigration Department. Often it is the licensing authority within a particular sector which will enforce the quotas, rather than the MHRE, for example, the Insurance Authority may (and does often) refuse to renew a licence unless the employer has met its quota.

A number of roles have also been reserved for UAE nationals. Businesses employing more than one hundred employees must engage a UAE national as Public or Government Relations Officer to liaise with the MHRE and the Immigration Department on sponsorship and employment issues. The roles of Human Resources Managers and Personnel Managers should also be filled by UAE nationals, and companies wishing to employ new secretaries must contact the TANMIA which will nominate UAE nationals for the post.

Often it is the licensing authority within a particular sector which will enforce the quotas, rather than the MHRE; for example, the Insurance Authority may (and does often) refuse to renew a licence unless the employer has met its quota.

In January 2017 additional reserved roles were announced, including the requirement for construction and industrial sector employers, with a workforce of five or more persons, to employ an Emirati health and safety officer, and companies employing one thousand or more employees to register the company on the MHRE's electronic system, Tasheel, and employ at least two Emirati employees to access that system.

TANMIA also monitors the application of quotas, and employers are obliged to supply information to TANMIA in July and January each year on their compliance. This authority aims to provide training to enhance the employability of UAE nationals, achieve full employment for UAE nationals, and replace a predominantly foreign workforce with a national one. The Emiratisation Council was also established to coordinate policy at a federal level, and the Khalifa Fund has been established to provide funds to private-sector employers in order to facilitate their employment of UAE nationals. TANMIA will often approach organizations within the private sector to initiate training programmes, internships and to create job opportunities for UAE nationals.

The MHRE, in 2010, introduced measures to encourage voluntary 'Emiratisation' by classifying employers registered with it according to specific criteria; with the employer's category determining the administrative fees and bank guarantees required for it to employ employees and to obtain work permits and residency visas. More recently Cabinet Decision No. 18/2022 on the classification of private-sector establishments was issued and came into effect on 1 June 2022. The new decision sets up a new system of classification for mainland private-sector companies, categorizing them into three groups depending on whether they meet the mandated Emiratisation rates, exceed such mandated rates, their percentage of skilled and unskilled workers, their commitment to a multicultural workforce, and adherence to the Labour Law and its Executive Regulations.

Emiratisation requirements do not apply in the DIFC and ADGM, and none of the free zones has an equivalent system for classifying employers as that operated by the MHRE. The DIFC Employment Law and ADGM Employment Regulations prohibit discrimination on the basis of sex, disability, marital status, race, nationality, religion, colour (ADGM only) age and pregnancy and maternity (DIFC only). However, these provisions apply to employees, and an employee is defined as an individual employed under an employment contract. Arguably therefore, an employer in the DIFC and ADGM may disregard potential discriminatory effects of any procedures or processes adopted as part of its recruitment procedures. The DIFC Employment Law and ADGM Employment Regulations do permit an employer to introduce programmes or activities to ameliorate the position of disadvantaged groups, and this could enable an employer to introduce programmes designed to increase the number of UAE nationals employed by its business.

3.2. RECRUITING

As set out above, there are no regulations regulating the procedures or processes an employer must follow in order to recruit foreign national employees. Foreign national employees will need to be sponsored for a work permit and residency visa purposes. Such sponsorship must be provided by a UAE-based employer and is employer specific, being granted usually for a period of two years.

When it comes to recruitment of UAE nationals, Ministerial Decree No. 212 of 2018 on Regulation of Employing Nationals in the Private Sector (the 'Emiratisation Decree') sets out requirements relating to the recruitment, ongoing support and termination of UAE nationals. Unemployed UAE nationals may apply for employment with any companies registered with the MHRE. Once they are successful, the decree prescribes various rules which must be followed in order to successfully employ the UAE national. This includes the requirement to secure the usual work permit. Once issued, the MHRE will issue the employee with an employment pack. The decree provides for UAE national employees to be employed on a two-year employment contract (which may be renewed by mutual agreement) and for the MHRE to make available to the UAE national training programmes relevant to his or her role and in line with market requirements. Under the MHRE's Ministerial Decision No. 52 of 1989 (Article 6), an employer is responsible for the costs associated with sponsorship and of bringing the employee to the UAE at the beginning of employment and of repatriating him or her upon the termination of employment. In exceptional circumstances, the flight costs can be borne by the employee, usually only if the employment is terminated during a probationary period or if the termination is due to the employee's actions (e.g., resignation or gross misconduct).

The Labour Law, the DIFC Employment Law and ADGM Employment Regulations specifically prohibit a recruitment business or agency from charging an employee a fee for its recruitment services. However, the DIFC Employment Law does permit employers to recuperate reasonable recruitment costs or expenses where the employee terminates their employment contract within the initial six-month period from commencement, subject to certain conditions being met.

The onus has traditionally been on employers to bring employees to the UAE and ensure they return to their home country on termination of the employment.

3.3. EMPLOYMENT APPLICATIONS

There are no specific legislative provisions regarding processing employment applications or considering them. The duty to employ UAE nationals and to recruit them is set out above.

Most employers will adopt a streamlined process applicable across their operations in all jurisdictions, with standard application forms, interview format and questioning.

3.4. PRE-EMPLOYMENT INQUIRIES

There is no legislation restricting the information an employer may request from an employee. The information gained must be held in accordance with data protection legislation and privacy rules.

3.5. PRE-EMPLOYMENT TESTS AND EXAMINATIONS

These are sector based and at the employer's discretion. As part of the sponsorship application process, an employee is required to undergo a medical examination, including a blood test for contagious diseases such as Human Immunodeficiency Viruses (HIV) and Hepatitis (strands B and C) and an X-ray testing for Tuberculosis (TB). Women may also be tested for pregnancy. If an employee tests positive for infectious disease, he or she would be required to leave the UAE. Certain nationalities may be required by the MHRE to complete medical tests prior to entry into the UAE. Such individuals would still have to undergo medical tests once in the UAE.

3.6. BACKGROUND, REFERENCE AND CREDIT CHECKS

The Labour Law does not impose any limitations on employers that wish to check the employment references and information presented by applicants. UAE residents are able to obtain Certificates of Good Conduct from the UAE police, and these may be requested from applicants as part of a selection process. An individual would only be able to obtain a Certificate of Good Conduct if he or she had lived in the UAE for at least six months. An equivalent certificate from the employee's home country can be requested confirming that the employee is free of a criminal conviction. As part of the work authorization process, an individual will undergo security checks. If the individual is to carry out work for a government authority through his or her employer, then additional checks and clearances will be required.

It is standard practice for an employee to be required to submit at least two references, and if he or she is to be employed in the financial services sector, then a credit check may be requested. Any information gained from such a check must be held in confidence, and the employee informed of such processing.

The DIFC and ADGM have data protection legislation, which must be adhered to with respect to any request for personal data from an employee.

Following termination of employment, an employee has the right to request the former employer to provide a factual reference certificate under Article 13 of the Labour Law. This certificate should set out: (i) the period of employment; (ii) the nature of work performed by the employee; and (iii) details of the employee's remuneration package.

Beyond this requirement, employers are not legally bound to issue references for former employees. Where an employer issues a reference, it should be mindful that making defamatory remarks is a criminal offence under the Crimes and Penalties Law in the UAE. An employer should also bear in mind that a reference may give rise to a claim in tort from the new or prospective employer or the former employee.

3.7. INTERVIEWING

There is no obligation to interview employees prior to offering them jobs. There is also no specific legislation in this area governing the format of an interview, questions to be avoided or which must be asked. Due to sponsorship processes, it is common to ask candidates if they are married or single, and in some instances, their age. However, an employer in the DIFC or ADGM would need to be mindful of the prohibition of discrimination (sex, marital status, race, nationality, religion, disability and age, pregnancy and maternity (DIFC only) and colour (ADGM only)). The DIFC Employment Law and ADGM Employment Regulations prohibit discrimination based on an individual being within one of the defined protected classes, whether direct or indirect, as well as the harassment of an individual due to being within a protected class. However, note the issue of whether the discrimination provisions cover candidates or only employees.

In common with other employee processes, many employers will operate a standard process across their multi-jurisdictional operations determined by company needs and business unit structures.

3.8.   HIRING PROCEDURES

Historically, employee remuneration and benefits packages have been determined on the basis of whether the employee is classed as 'single' or 'married/accompanied'. The use of such status stems from employers sourcing labour needs from outside the UAE and enabling employees to bring their spouses and/or children to the UAE with them.

Once an employee is extended an offer of employment, the sponsorship application process must be commenced. The employee is required to provide copies of his professional and educational certificates which must be attested and authenticated in the country where the issuing institution is. This process is designed to ensure that the documents are genuine and involves the certificates being stamped as authentic by the UAE embassy and Ministry of Foreign Affairs and International Cooperation.

Once the application is accepted, the MHRE will issue an entry permit, permitting the employee to enter the UAE on the basis of employment. Once in the UAE, the sponsorship application process must be completed within sixty days during which the employee cannot leave the UAE, or the process is invalidated. The free zone authorities follow a similar model to this process.

3.9.   FINES AND PENALTIES

A fine will be payable if the sponsorship application process is not completed within sixty days of the employee entering the UAE on an entry permit.

If an employer-based 'onshore' is found to have charged an employee a fee for recruitment or passed on recruitment costs to the employee, the employer can be fined AED 5,000 for each employee.

3.10. CHECKLIST OF DO'S AND DON'TS

- Obtain references and criminal record checks for all new employees.
- Require employees to submit authenticated and attested professional and educational certificates.
- Execute the standard form of MHRE documents.
- Comply with the immigration timeframes.
- Carry out credit checks for employees engaged in financial or accounting roles.
- Hold all information in strict confidence, inform employees of the information collected, and how it will be held.

4. MANAGING PERFORMANCE/CONDUCT

4.1. OVERVIEW

There are no specific regulations regarding performance management procedures. However, the Labour Law together with the Executive Regulations regulate disciplinary processes and the disciplinary sanctions which may be imposed. The Labour Law does not distinguish between poor performance and misconduct in terms of the required process and potential sanctions. The DIFC Employment Law and ADGM Employment Regulations oblige every employer to have written disciplinary and grievance procedures.

The use of formal performance management or performance improvement plans varies from employer to employer and depends on the sophistication of the employer's internal processes and in many instances how integrated the employer is across its operations globally. Certain sectors or roles will lend themselves more easily to performance plans as employees in sales roles or who are remunerated on commission and/or bonus will often be subject to early warnings or indicators of poor performance.

4.2. COACHING AND COUNSELLING

There is no requirement to provide coaching or counselling for a poorly performing employee, and such coaching or counselling will not be necessary in order to render a termination for poor performance fair. Employers' practices in this area differ and larger multinational employers will often apply performance improvement plans providing for mentoring, coaching and counselling. However, where the employee is a UAE national, an employer's ability to terminate the employment is restricted, and certain additional steps may be required. The MHRE will expect an employer to have provided a UAE national employee with coaching, support and training to perform the role before termination for poor performance or misconduct can be considered.

4.3. WRITTEN EVALUATIONS

Appraisals or written evaluations are widely used in order to assess employees' performance. Such documents can be used in order to justify an employee termination for poor performance, provided the written documents set out clearly any performance concerns and the actions the employer may take in response if no improvement is made.

4.4. WARNINGS AND SUSPENSIONS

Under the Labour Law and Executive Regulations, an employer must follow a minimum procedure involving setting out the performance concerns in writing, meeting with the employee to hear his representations regarding the concerns, and then confirming any decision in writing. Recognized disciplinary sanctions include written warnings, denial of promotions, denial of a salary increase, financial penalty, and suspension without pay for a maximum permitted period of fourteen days.

4.5. CHECKLIST OF DO'S AND DON'TS

– If a company has policies and procedures regarding assessing performance or addressing poor performance, then these should be followed. Failure to do so could lead to a complaint being raised by the employee.
– Ensure that procedures are documented and warnings are issued in writing.
– If termination is a possibility, this should be communicated in writing and clearly expressed.

5. TERMINATION OF EMPLOYEES FOR PERFORMANCE OR DISCIPLINARY REASONS

5.1. OVERVIEW

The Labour Law sets out the circumstances in which a contract of employment may be terminated by either party and the circumstances in which an employer may dismiss an employee without notice.

An employment contract can be terminated in any of the following circumstances:

– if the parties agree to terminate the contract, provided that the employee consents to this in writing;
– if the contract term has come to an end (unless the contract has been explicitly or implicitly amended);
– by one of the parties subject to observing the statutory notice requirements.

Either party may terminate the contract for a legitimate reason by serving written notice of termination which must be a minimum of thirty days and a maximum of ninety days, as contractually agreed.

An employee loses the entitlement to notice if he or she is terminated 'for cause' under Article 44 of the Labour Law. The exhaustive list of circumstances in which 'cause' will exist justifying summary dismissal is as follows:

– If the employee adopts a false identity or nationality or submits forged certificates or documents.
– If the employee makes a mistake that causes the employer to suffer substantial material loss.
– If the employee violates instructions for workplace health and safety.
– If the employee fails to carry out basic duties, as provided in the employment contract, after receiving three written warnings from the employer.
– If the employee divulges confidential information which results in losses to the employer.
– If the employee is found in a state of drunkenness or under the influence of a drug during working hours.
– If, while working, the employee assaults the employer, the responsible manager, or any of his or her work mates.
– If the employee is absent from work without a valid reason for more than seven consecutive days or twenty intermittent days in any one year.
– If the employee illegally exploits his position for personal gain.

– If the employee joins another employer without complying with the termination rules.

There is no equivalent list in the DIFC Employment Law and the ADGM Employment Regulations. An employer is entitled to terminate an employee without notice or the payment of statutory severance pay under the ADGM Employment Regulations if the employee is guilty of misbehaviour, defined as circumstances in which a reasonable employer would terminate employment summarily. Under the DIFC Employment Law, both the employer and the employee are permitted to terminate the contractual relationship where the conduct of one party warrants termination and where a reasonable employer or employee would have terminated the employment as a consequence. The difference being is that where the employer terminated for cause, the employee is not entitled to receive wages in lieu of notice but will receive payment of statutory severance pay and accrued unused annual leave calculated up to the termination date. Where the employee terminates, the employee is entitled to receive wages in lieu of notice, severance pay and accrued unused annual leave calculated to include the notice period. Aside from the Article 44 circumstances, an employer may dismiss an employee at any time during the employment by serving contractual notice of termination. There is no list of 'legitimate' reasons for termination with notice. The Labour Law requires that the employer pays the employee all dues within fourteen days of termination.

The concept of arbitrary dismissal is no longer provided for under the Labour Law. However, in instances where an employee is terminated due to the successful filing of a complaint or a labour claim with the MHRE/labour court, such-and-such termination is ruled unlawful, the employer may be required to pay compensation to the employee of up to three months of remuneration. In determining the amount of compensation the court will consider the type of work, damage sustained and length of service. A foreign employee who raises a claim will be entitled to maintain his UAE residency visa until the conclusion of the claim and may be issued with a temporary work permit to permit him to take up alternative employment.

The Labour Law together with the Executive Regulations contain a disciplinary code, and various disciplinary penalties that an employer may impose on employees. The code includes a basic disciplinary procedure that should be followed before any disciplinary penalty is imposed upon an employee. This procedure requires the employer to notify the employee in writing of the charges against him or her, meet with the employee and investigate any defence raised by the employee. The employee must then be advised in writing of the disciplinary outcome and apprised of the penalties that will be imposed in the event of a repeat offence. An employer must initiate the disciplinary procedure within thirty days of discovering the misconduct, and the disciplinary sanction must be imposed within sixty days of the investigation being concluded and the employee's guilt being established. Strictly speaking, an employer applying its own disciplinary code should obtain the MHRE's approval to do so, but in practice, such approval is rarely sought. Provided employers comply with the minimum provisions of the Labour Law regarding due process and the imposition of disciplinary sanctions, they will not be in violation.

The DIFC Employment Law and ADGM Employment Regulations do not contain an equivalent concept of arbitrary dismissal or any provisions regarding unfair dismissal. Any complaints regarding the enforcement or application of the DIFC Employment Law or the ADGM Employment Regulations should be made to the DIFC Authority or ADGM Board (as applicable) which have the responsibility of enforcing such laws. In the DIFC, employment complaints are currently being directed to the Small Claims Tribunal which initiates a conciliation process; and then refers claims for full hearings or to the Court of First Instance depending on the value of the claim and its complexity. It is also possible for an employee to raise a claim directly in the Court of First Instance. The Small Claims Tribunal is able to deal with claims valued at AED 100,000 or up to AED 500,000, provided both parties agree to its jurisdiction. Within ADGM, employment disputes will initially be heard in the ADGM Commercial Court; however, ultimately it is envisaged that a separate labour court will be established with its own set of procedural rules.

The ADGM Board of Directors and the DIFC Authority have the capacity to introduce regulations to facilitate the administration of the ADGM Employment Regulations and the DIFC Employment Law (respectively) or which furthers their purpose.

An employer in the DIFC or ADGM could potentially face a claim of discrimination on prohibited grounds if an employee claimed that the termination was due to his or her membership of one of the protected groups defined in the relevant law.

5.2.   SEPARATION/SEVERANCE PAY

In addition to notice pay, pay in lieu of accrued but unused holidays, and any other contractual sums due to an employee upon termination of employment, the Labour Law provides that certain employees may be entitled to receive severance pay commonly known as 'end of service gratuity'.

Generally, if an employee has more than one year of continuous service, he or she will be entitled to severance pay of up to twenty-one days of basic wages for every year of the first five years of service, and thirty days of basic wages for every year thereafter (provided the payment does not exceed two years of wage in total). The entitlement to severance pay is pro-rated for partial years worked once the initial year of service is attained. The reference to days is to calendar days.

Severance pay is calculated according to the last basic wage paid to the employee and is payable upon the termination or expiry of the contract of employment. Allowances and benefits are excluded from the calculation. However, payments such as bonus or commission may be included, depending on the terms for making such payments and the express provisions of the employment contract.

The Labour Law also requires employers to repatriate non-UAE national employees upon the termination of their employment. The obligation is to purchase their travel ticket to return them to their original country, subject to any more generous contractual arrangements in place. The obligation to repatriate will transfer to a new employer if the employee takes up alternative employment following termination of employment with the original employer.

The ADGM Employment Regulations also include an entitlement to severance pay calculated in the same way as under the Labour Law. However, there is no reduction in the entitlement if an employee resigns during the first five years of employment. Under the ADGM Employment Regulations, this entitlement is calculated solely on basic salary (excluding all allowances, benefits in kind, bonus and commission). Employees on fixed-term contracts are not treated differently to those on unlimited-term contracts for the purposes of severance pay.

The DIFC Authority has replaced the previous arrangement of end of service gratuity, payable on termination of employment, with a defined contribution savings scheme, in which contributions are made monthly into a scheme called a Qualifying Scheme. The Qualifying Scheme which is being supported by the DIFC Authority is the DIFC Employee Workplace Savings (DEWS) plan; however, employers may choose to use a Qualifying Alternative Scheme or obtain an exemption in relation to another Qualifying Scheme. End of service gratuity ceased to accrue after 31 January 2020 and employers are obliged to make monthly contributions into DEWS or other Qualifying Scheme from 1 February 2020. However, employers were given until 30 April 2020 to enrol in the scheme.

End of service gratuity accrued up to and including 31 January 2020 (Accrued Gratuity) will not be lost and will instead be paid out following the termination of the employee's employment (calculated based on the employee's basic salary as at the termination date). Alternatively, employees may consent to the employer transferring the employee's Accrued Gratuity into DEWS.

The DIFC Employment Law permits the employer and employee to enter into a settlement agreement to resolve a dispute / terminate an employment contract, provided that the settlement agreement is in writing, and that the employee has had the opportunity to receive independent legal advice on the issue. The ADGM Employment Regulations do not preclude parties from entering into a settlement agreement and waiving claims against each other.

The Labour Law does not include any specific provisions regulating the use of separation agreements or statutory requirements dictating the contents or form of such agreements. Use of such agreements, however, is common in the UAE. Such agreements do not act as a bar to the employee raising a complaint but are strong written evidence of the employee's acceptance of defined terms and payments on termination of the employment. Enforceability of such agreements may be enhanced if the agreement is signed in front of a Notary Public.

Generally, the most effective way to avoid litigation by non-UAE national employees in the event of their termination is to offer them a settlement in return for their cooperation with the cancellation of their work permit and, thereafter, their UAE residence visa. In order to cancel an employee's work permit, the employee is required to sign an acknowledgement form called an End of Service Entitlement Form, stating that he or she received all sums due from the employer and that he or she has no claims against the employer. This declaration is generally taken by the authorities to be a waiver or acknowledgement by the employee that no claims exist against the employer. However, the employee signing it does not bar him from bringing a claim later in the Courts on the basis that he was not paid his entitlements.

5.3. FINES AND PENALTIES

The concept of arbitrary dismissal is no longer provided for under the Labour Law. However, in instances where an employee is terminated due to the successful filing of a complaint or a labour claim with the MHRE/labour court, and such termination is ruled unlawful, the employer may be required to pay compensation to the employee of up to three months of remuneration. In determining the amount of compensation the court will consider the type of work, damage sustained and length of service. If an employer was found to have compelled an employee to acknowledge in writing that he or she had received all dues arising out of the employment when this was untrue, the employer could be liable to a fine of between AED 5,000 and AED 1,000,000.

Under the DIFC Employment Law where the court considers that there has been a contravention, it may order the respondent to pay compensation up to an amount equivalent to the employee's annual wage (which may be doubled in instances where the employer does not comply with the court's order). Potential liability under the ADGM Employment Regulations is unclear. For a discrimination claim in the ADGM, it is possible that a claim could be based on a breach of contract claim and an employee could argue for loss of earnings suffered as a result of the discriminatory act. An employee could also claim compensation on the basis that the discriminatory act is a statutory tort.

5.4.   CHECKLIST OF DO'S AND DON'TS

– Always document poor performance or misconduct.
– Comply with internal disciplinary and performance management procedures.
– Consider any potential discriminatory impact of performance assessment measures and any potential for a termination to be unfair or discriminatory.
– Set out the reason for dismissal in the termination letter.
– Document final payments made to an employee, calculation methods, and obtain employee sign off.

6.   LAYOFFS, REDUCTIONS IN FORCE AND/OR REDUNDANCIES AS A RESULT OF JOB ELIMINATIONS OR OTHER RESTRUCTURING

6.1.   OVERVIEW

The Labour Law does not contain any provisions governing workforce reductions and does not recognize the concept of 'redundancy' but does recognize termination due to permanent closure of the establishment.

That said, the UAE courts have recognized an employer's entitlement to restructure and reorganize its business, with the consequence that overheads may be cut or roles eliminated, thereby resulting in termination of employment. However, this is an unclear area of law. Court decisions have made it clear that a high evidentiary burden will be imposed on an employer seeking to justify an employment termination by reason of redundancy and often business decisions made by an employer will be relevant, for example, the existence of a genuine redundancy when the business is spending money refitting its premises or taking out new office space, whether the restructure involves a group of employees or only one. It is harder to justify making one employee redundant as it appears to be 'cherry picking' rather than the redundancy of the role. Note that any successful defence of redundancy termination must involve headcount reduction. The Labour Courts are also reluctant to accept a redundancy termination as being genuine where the sole purpose of the termination appears to be to increase the profit of the employer. Evidentially, it can be helpful for an employer to produce structural charts both prior to and post-reorganization.

In the absence of such legislative provisions, some employers have chosen to introduce redundancy policies regulating how the company will determine whether a role is redundant and when a redundancy situation exists, identifying business units within the company or groups of employees if potential redundancies are to be identified, and redundancy selection criteria if employees are to be selected for redundancy out of a group of employees. Such policies can also cover the process of locating alternative employment within the business for redundant employees.

When terminating UAE nationals, the Emiratisation Decree (Ministerial Decree No. 212 of 2018 on Regulation of Employing Nationals in the Private Sector – refer to section 3.2) requires the employer to conduct an exit interview with the UAE national employee prior to any termination. The employer is then required to submit an 'exit interview' report to the MHRE.

6.2. REDUCTIONS IN FORCE/LAYOFFS/JOB ELIMINATIONS

In the absence of legislative provisions, reductions in work hours, variations in work patterns and sabbaticals or absence without pay or reduced pay are all matters for contractual negotiation and agreement with individual employees. Such measures were introduced by a number of employers in 2009 at the height of the economic crisis. If a contractual variation is agreed of this nature then the registered contract with the MHRE or the free zone would need to be updated, as it is the operative contract as far as the UAE authorities are concerned, and if it continued to state a higher rate of remuneration or work pattern then this would continue to apply.

6.3. FINES AND PENALTIES

There is no requirement for reporting business reorganizations or restructuring resulting in redundancies or mass layoffs; nor is there a requirement to inform and consult regarding redundancy proposals; accordingly, no fines or penalties apply for failure to take any of these measures.

When a business makes redundancy terminations, the potential fine or penalty is the exposure to claims by employees for illegitimate termination; however, given that the concept of arbitrary dismissal is no longer provided for under the Labour Law, it remains to be seen how the courts will approach such claims. If a UAE national is terminated unlawfully. Pursuant to the

Emiratisation Decree (Decree No. 212 of 2018 – refer to section 3.2), the MHRE may implement any of the following measures:

(a) A fine of AED 20,000 for breach of the Decree.
(b) The MHRE can direct the company to reinstate the employee if it considers that the termination was arbitrary and if the company refuses, the MHRE can impose a fine of AED 20,000.

6.4.   CHECKLIST OF DO'S AND DON'TS

– Always document the termination procedure and reason for dismissal.
– Consider adopting a redundancy policy as a matter of company policy.
– Follow personnel best practice in adopting a process to explain to employees the redundancy situation and its effect on the business.
– When selecting an employee for redundancy out of a group of employees, have a clear and documented process for selecting this employee out of many.
– Follow the termination procedure for UAE nationals.

7.   LABOUR AND EMPLOYMENT LAW RAMIFICATIONS UPON ACQUISITION OR SALE OF BUSINESS

7.1.   OVERVIEW

There are no legislative provisions providing for an immediate and automatic transfer of employees upon the acquisition or sale of a business, nor is there any duty to inform and consult or provide specific information to employees when a business is being sold or acquired.

That said, Article 48 of the Labour Law provides for continuity of employment where the legal form or position of the employer changes, for example, from a partnership to a limited liability company. Pursuant to such provision, the new employer is required to adhere to the terms of the employee's employment contract as well as the Labour Law and Executive Regulations from the date the change is made. In practice, the MHRE and the Labour Courts will often interpret Article 48 of the Labour Law broadly to apply to transactions whereby employees are moved from one employing entity to another whether pursuant to a corporate restructure or the sale of a business unit.

On a general note, due diligence regarding labour and employment matters can often be overlooked in this region when considering whether or not to acquire a business. Such oversights lead to practical difficulties once a business is acquired and potentially the company taking on liabilities it had not envisaged.

7.2.   ACQUISITION OF A BUSINESS

Clearly, acquisition through a share purchase does not affect the employees who continue being employed by the same entity on the same terms and conditions and are simply inherited by the purchaser. There is also a largely untested ministerial resolution providing for the licence of a branch of one entity to be taken over by another, which if successfully applied for, could result in the automatic movement of employees pursuant to the takeover of the licence.

If a part of a business is bought as a going concern, then the issue of employees employed in that part of the business is a matter for the seller and purchaser to agree as part of the commercial transaction. The purchaser may be concerned to secure the transfer of the employees in order to be able to continue running the business acquired. Alternatively, there may be a need for only some or even none of the employees, meaning that the new employer will want to cherry-pick those employees it takes on and those who remain with the old employer; who may, in turn, make such employees redundant.

The technical employment position in such a situation is that of 'termination and rehire'. If the employees are to follow the sale of the business, then the current employer selling the business must terminate the employment, and the purchaser of the business must rehire the employees. Given that the law does not provide for a seamless automatic transition from seller to purchaser, the 'termination and rehire' mechanism means that employment entitlements will crystallize on termination of employment by the seller; meaning that the seller will become liable for entitlements arising on termination. The main entitlements on termination are the end of service gratuity under the Labour Law (this benefit being replicated under the DIFC Employment Law and ADGM Employment Regulations), the right to at least one month's written notice of termination and payment in lieu of accrued untaken holiday.

Depending on the commercial context of the sale (often whether it is a multi-jurisdictional acquisition or a local UAE one), the seller and purchaser may agree that where possible any entitlements arising on termination of employment are not paid out but 'rolled over' to the new employment with the purchaser. Such an agreement must be implemented with employee consent and is a matter of contractual agreement with each employee on an individual basis. There are broadly three options with regard to accrued employee entitlements arising at the point of transfer: (i) to pay out all accrued entitlements; (ii) to roll over all accrued entitlements; or (iii) to pay out all accrued entitlements but for the new employer to recognize the past service for the purposes of accrual of entitlements, i.e., to recognize seniority.

Another general point is that the rehire of employees will likely have to be on the same or more favourable terms and conditions of employment; otherwise, employees are unlikely to accept employment on less favourable terms. Employees who are left with the seller and not offered employment with the purchaser will have to be re-allocated or redeployed within the business, or else made redundant.

7.3.   ACQUISITION CHECKLIST

– A purchaser should always carry out due diligence on the employees it will inherit, the status of such employees and the status of the business with the MHRE (i.e., what classification of the employer the business falls into, whether it has registered violations and fines), Immigration Department and Pensions Authority.
– Accrued liability for end of service gratuity should be investigated and also whether such liability has been recorded in the businesses' accounts and records (including whether or not funds have been allocated for the liability) in accordance with the requirements under the Commercial Companies Law (Law No. 2 of 2015, as amended).
– Due diligence should also cover the key terms and conditions of employees (particularly senior management) and identify any unusual terms and conditions of employment, for example, benefits cover, commission arrangements and bonus arrangements. Employees' nationalities should also be requested as well as each employee's visa status.
– Due diligence should also identify whether any employees are international assignees, with underlying employment contracts in another jurisdiction or if employees are dual contract employees, having a local UAE contract and also a contract with an offshore holding company or 'mother' company. Such arrangements give potential scope for dual claims.
– Due diligence should cover any current or potential disputes with employees and the existence or otherwise of post-termination restrictions in key personnel's contracts.
– If the business is being bought in its entirety (through share purchase), a purchaser should ensure that the trade license of the business covers the activities the employees are carrying out and the actual business being conducted.

7.4.   SALE OF A BUSINESS

In the absence of legislative provisions providing for automatic transfer of employees by operation of law on the sale of a business either in part or in whole, as a going concern (e.g., through a service provision change or sale of assets and other commercial interests, for example, goodwill, property lease, etc.) and in the absence of a duty to inform and consult with employees, a seller does not have a great deal of compliance considerations on the sale of a business, compared to many other jurisdictions. However, it may be that the employment situation of the business necessitates that the commercial terms of the sale be adjusted and the sale price reduced. It is also not uncommon for a seller to agree to meet 50% of any liability arising out of employee terminations or otherwise within six months of the sale. Depending on the commercial agreement, it may be that the seller incurs the full liability for employee entitlements arising on termination if these employees are to be moved to the purchaser through a 'termination and rehire' mechanism. Alternatively, if the seller is to meet the costs of redundancies following the sale of the business, then the sale price and the commercial terms will need to reflect this liability.

7.5.   SALE CHECKLIST

- A seller will need to know whether the purchaser intends to take on any of the employees currently employed within the business being sold and the terms and conditions on offer to employees.
- Consider reflecting the liabilities the seller will face (e.g., having to make redundancies post-sale or to pay out accrued employment entitlements on completion) in the commercial terms and the sale price.

8.   USE OF ALTERNATIVE WORKFORCES: INDEPENDENT CONTRACTORS, CONTRACT EMPLOYEES, TEMPORARY OR LEASED WORKERS AND PART-TIME OR VOLUNTARY WORKERS

8.1.   OVERVIEW

The lawful use of independent contractors, contract employees, temporary or leased workers has historically been severely restricted under the Labour Law and generally in the UAE. With a largely expatriate workforce, the majority of individuals working in the UAE require sponsorship for a work permit and residency visa purposes. Such sponsorship is based on employee status and is employer (and location) specific. Historically individuals (regardless of nationality) claiming self-employed status must hold a trade license to carry out business in their own right (as any commercial activity is required to be licensed in the UAE). A trade license covers specific activities, and the individual must ensure that his or her license covers the activities they wish to provide.

A recent exception to this, are those who have received Golden Visas, being long-term residence visas, which enable foreigners to live, work and study in the UAE without the need to be sponsored by an employer/company. These visas are issued to select professionals and talented individuals for a term of either five or ten years (renewable automatically). The Executive Regulations have further introduced various new types of work permits, including work permits for those who hold a Golden Visa and Freelance permits for self-employed individuals (who have their own sponsorship, usually by being sponsored as dependants by relatives, having their own trade licence or freelance licence from a free zone).

Employment businesses are uncommon in the UAE, and the authorities do not generally grant trade licenses permitting the engagement of individuals by an agency which in turn supplies those individuals to its clients or 'end users'. Where such organizations have been able to obtain the requisite trade license, the agency itself is the employer of the individuals supplied and incurs full liability as an employer for those individuals. Under Ministerial Resolution No. 1283 of 2010 regarding the licensing and regulation of private recruitment agencies, such licenses are only granted to UAE nationals, and the business must have a UAE national holding a university degree acting as its General Manager.

8.2.   INDEPENDENT CONTRACTORS

8.2.1.   Definition

An independent contractor will be an individual holding his own trade license permitting him to supply the services he is contracting to offer. A standard term of an independent contractor agreement would be to include an indemnity to the effect that the contractor has a valid license to supply the services he is contracting to provide. There is no statutory definition of a contractor, but given the immigration requirements for expatriate workers and the requirement for all employees to be registered as such with the MHRE or a free zone authority (as appropriate), it follows that any legitimate and lawful contractor will be one with a trade license to act in his own independent capacity.

8.2.2. Creating the Relationship

The relationship would be created through commercial agreement and a written contract. Strictly speaking, a written contract may not be necessary, and an oral contract may be evidenced through conduct. However, in the interests of clarity and to avoid disputes, a written contract would be advisable. The terms of the contract should be indicative of a commercial relationship and one where the contractor is in business on his own account and thereby taking on some element of commercial risk.

8.2.3. Compensation

There are no legislative provisions regarding compensation. However, in keeping with a commercial relationship, compensation for services should be based on delivery and not on time or per-hour basis.

8.2.4. Other Terms and Conditions

An independent contractor's agreement should also provide for access to the worksite (as appropriate), supply or substitution or personnel, notices, indemnities, insurance cover, supply or payment for equipment and tools, and health and safety.

8.3. CONTRACT WORKERS

There is no statutory definition of contract workers. All employees under the Labour Law are required to be on fixed-term employment contract of up to a maximum term of three years. Contract workers are generally engaged for a specific task or duration. Such workers have full employment status and entitlements. As stated above the maximum permitted duration of a fixed-term contract is three years

The expiry of a fixed-term contract in itself does not amount to an actionable termination. Either party may terminate the contract for a legitimate reason on service of written notice which must be a minimum of thirty days and a maximum of ninety days, as contractually agreed.

8.4.   LEASED WORKERS

Provided an employee has been employed by his employer for at least one year, the MHRE permits the leasing of the employee to another employer for a period of six months. Specific permission must be obtained from the MHRE for such an arrangement, and the six-month temporary work permit may be renewed for a further six months. Such an arrangement is not the equivalent of an employment business scheme whereby temporary workers or temporary employment services are provided.

In some instances, for example, for the provision of IT services, it is not uncommon for a business to contract with another business for the provision of certain professional services; the supply of personnel to provide those services would be ancillary to the commercial agreement. In such a situation, the personnel could be regarded as being 'leased'. There would not be deemed employment of the leased workers by the end user of those services. However, the business to whom the workers are being supplied could face potential sanction if an MHRE inspection was conducted, and the Labour Inspector regarded the arrangements as an illegitimate supply of labour and a violation of immigration regulations (which provide that an employee may only work for the entity which sponsors him for work permit and residency visa purposes). In order to avoid potential fines, approval for the arrangement can be sought from the Labour Relations department of the MHRE.

The MHRE will grant temporary work permits of six months' duration (which are renewable), enabling employees to be seconded from one company to another. These permits can enable employees to be seconded into another company in the same or another emirate within the UAE, provided that the company is also registered with the MHRE.

In limited circumstances where a company has a contract for services with another company, the MHRE's Labour Relations Department will stamp or attest the agreement to permit the ancillary provision of employees to the second company in order for the services to be performed or provided.

8.5.   PART-TIME AND VOLUNTARY EMPLOYMENT

Ministerial Resolution No. 31 of 2018, which came into force on 1 March 2018, introduced a part-time employment system enabling companies to recruit employees on a part-time basis, either within or outside the UAE. It also enables employees to work on a part-time basis for more than one employer without having to obtain the consent of their primary employer, subject to a work permit being obtained by each employer. In order to qualify for such work permits, employees must possess a minimum diploma qualification.

Within the Emirate of Dubai, Law No. 5 of 2018 regulating the volunteering activity in Dubai was issued in April 2019 granting the Dubai Community Development Authority the responsibility for overseeing voluntary work arrangements and setting up a volunteering register within the Emirate.

8.6.   CHECKLIST OF DO'S AND DON'TS

– Ensure that all contract workers have proper work permits and permission to work for the company.
– Ensure contract workers have clear contracts with start and end dates.
– Ensure that independent contractors are properly licensed to provide the services being offered.
– Ensure that any leased or supplied workers are lawfully working within the business.

9.   OBLIGATION TO BARGAIN COLLECTIVELY WITH TRADE UNIONS: EMPLOYEES' RIGHT TO STRIKE AND A COMPANY'S RIGHT TO CONTINUE BUSINESS OPERATIONS

9.1.   OVERVIEW OF UNIONS' RIGHT TO ORGANIZE

Trade unions, collective associations, workers' councils and the like are unlawful in the UAE. However, the MHRE offers employees a dispute resolution mechanism whereby complaints from employees may be submitted collectively in writing to the MHRE. The complaint must be filed within two weeks of the date of the dispute. The MHRE may then mediate between the employees and the employer to resolve the dispute. If this process does not achieve a settlement, the MHRE will refer the matter to the Collective Labour Disputes Committee, which is a special body established by the MHRE. The Collective Labour Disputes Committee shall settle the dispute. Their decision shall be final and sealed with the executory formula seal by the competent court.

It is unlawful to strike in the UAE and a criminal offence under the UAE Crimes and Penalties Law. Employees are permitted to form welfare committees overseen by the employer and to administer social funds in consultation with the employer. However, there is no entitlement to associate. Where collective labour disputes do emerge, the MHRE will attempt to act as a mediator. However, it is not uncommon for employees who have participated in a strike or demonstration to face mass deportation.

10. WORKING CONDITIONS: HOURS OF WORK AND PAYMENT OF WAGES – BY STATUTE OR COLLECTIVE AGREEMENTS

10.1. OVERVIEW OF WAGE AND HOURS LAWS

The Labour Law together with the Executive Regulations provide that employees shall be paid their wage on their due date as stated in the employment contract, in UAE Dirhams (unless a different currency is agreed contractually) and through the Wage Protection System (WPS).

If there is a shortfall in wage payments made to an employee, he or she can raise a complaint with the MHRE or relevant free zone authority, as applicable.

An employer who repeatedly fails to pay employees may be liable to a fine between AED 5,000 and AED 50,000 under Cabinet Decision No. 21/2020 on the fees of services and administrative penalties at the MHRE and a fine between AED 5,000 and AED 1,000,000 under the Labour Law, as well as other sanctions as set out under Ministerial Decision No. 43/2022 regarding the wage protection system ('WPS Decree').

Electronic Wages Protection System

The WPS Decree came into effect in February 2022, repealing the previously issued EPS Ministerial Decrees, which initially established the Wages Protection System (WPS) which has been in place since 1 September 2009. The WPS is overseen by a dedicated WPS office within the MHRE and is designed to ensure transparency in the payment process, and that employees are paid on time. The system provides for the following:

(1) That employees are paid at least once each month:
   (a) The WPS office has a list of approved institutions (a bank, money exchange, or service provider registered and approved by the UAE Central Bank) through which payment of wages by employers may be made.
   (b) The employer chooses one of the approved institutions through which to make wage payments to employees under WPS.
   (c) The employer supplies its selected institution with details of all wages payable to employees (payroll information).

(d) The selected institution sends this information to the WPS office, which then compares this information with the details it holds for the employer's registered employees.

(e) No deduction for charges by way of bank fees or transfer fees may be made to payments due to employees.

The WPS Decree imposes the following key provisions:

(1) All establishments registered with MHRE must pay their employees through the WPS.

(2) If the wage is not paid within fifteen days of the due date, the payment will be considered late (unless specified otherwise in the employment contract) and penalties will be imposed according to the table set out under Article 2 of the law.

(3) Companies are considered compliant with WPS where they pay a minimum of 90% of their workforce through WPS.

(4) Employees are considered to be in receipt of their salary where they receive a minimum of 80% of their wage as set out in their employment contract provided proof of deduction is produced on request.

(5) Any agreement to a period of unpaid leave must be communicated to the MHRE.

(6) The following employee categories are excluded from WPS:
   (a) employees who have filed a wage complaint with the Labour Court;
   (b) employees who have been reported to the Ministry as absent;
   (c) new employees up to thirty days from their wage due date; and
   (d) employees on unpaid leave provided supporting documents are submitted to the Ministry.

(7) The following employer categories are excluded from WPS:
   (a) UAE national owned fishing boats;
   (b) UAE national owned public taxis;
   (c) banks; and
   (d) houses of worship.

Employers have a grace period of three months to comply (from 15 February 2022).

The system has historically caused issues for employers with international assignees or seconded employees who would usually be paid in their home country. The effect of the WPS is to require employers to split payroll for such employees. However, Article 22 of the Labour Law does permit the parties to contractually agree payment in another currency. The MHRE has in the past, prior to the current Labour Law being in effect, in exceptional circumstances, given clearance for an employee to be paid outside of the

WPS, but this usually required the employee to appear in person at the MHRE's WPS team, confirming in person and in writing that he continues to be paid and providing evidence of the payments.

Free Zones

Free zones are not within the MHRE's jurisdiction. Many were expected to put in place regulations imposing similar obligations regarding electronic transfer of wages. However, to date, few of them have done so. The JAFZA does impose a requirement on employers within its jurisdiction to provide salary certificates for each employee confirming each month that employees registered with the free zone authority have been made. It also started in later 2012 to require employers within its jurisdiction to apply the WPS. The Dubai Airport Free Zone Authority also in 2012 began requiring employers within its jurisdiction to submit salary certificates each month confirming that the employee has been paid.

Working Hours

The Labour Law states that the maximum normal hours of work in the UAE for adult employees shall be eight hours per day or forty-eight hours per week. Employees required to work on a shift basis are permitted to work a maximum of fifty-six hours per week.

Working hours are reduced by two hours each day during Ramadan, regardless of whether an employee is fasting or not. During the summer months of June to August, a mandatory afternoon ban on employees working outdoors in the midday sun is imposed, with violations being punishable by fines imposed by the MHRE. Employers must also provide employees with resting areas in shade, facilities and drinking water.

Young persons (those aged between 15 and 18 years) may not be required to work between 7:00 p.m. and 7:00 a.m. Young persons may work a maximum of six hours per day, which shall include one or more rest breaks, which shall amount to not less than one hour in total. Breaks must be arranged so that a young person works not more than four consecutive hours.

The DIFC Employment Law sets out a maximum permitted working week of forty-eight hours, averaged over a seven-day period. Employees are permitted to opt out of this maximum provided they do so in writing.

Other applicable rest periods under the DIFC Employment Law are eleven hours in a twenty-four-hour period, one day (twenty-four hours) of rest per week (over a seven-day period), one-hour rest in every six-hour period. Hours during Ramadan are only reduced for Muslim employees.

The working time provisions in the ADGM Employment Regulations require working time not to exceed an average of forty-eight hours for each seven-day period and the standard rest breaks provided for in the DIFC

Employment Law are replicated in the ADGM Employment Regulations. Muslim employees observing the fast are required to reduce their working hours by two hours per day.

10.2. MINIMUM WAGE

The Labour Law, the DIFC Employment Law and the ADGM Employment Regulations do not provide for a minimum wage. However, the DIFC Employment Law does provide that basic wage shall not be less than 50% of the employee's annual wage. Elsewhere, it has been a market practice in the UAE to divide remuneration into two headings: basic salary and allowances on the basis of a 60:40 ratio. The most common type of allowances is housing and transport, with more senior employees also receiving allowances for their children's school fees and club membership. Remuneration packages are also traditionally classed as 'accompanied' or 'unaccompanied', meaning that the employee's package is determined on the basis that he or she will or will not be accompanied by a spouse and or children.

An employee with a basic salary of less than approximately AED 4,000 is unable to sponsor dependants to live with him in the UAE.

Under Cabinet Resolution No. 26 of 2010, organizations which are rated 'First Class' by the MHRE (and consequently subject to less fees and restrictive bank guarantee requirements) must employ 20% of its workforce with the following recommended minimum wage according to their skill level:

– skill level 1 (Bachelor's Degree or higher): AED 12,000;
– skill level 2 (Diploma): AED 7,000;
– skill level 3 (secondary education): AED 5,000.

To benefit from the 'First Class' rating, the Emiratisation quota must be at least 15% of the total workers of the aforementioned skill levels.

As yet, the salary levels stipulated for each skill set are recommended and not compulsory. As such, they are designed to encourage compliance by employers and also the retention of a more educated workforce. Further, an employee may have a higher educational qualification than that required by the role actually carried out by him. His skill set will be judged to be the one for the role he is carrying out regardless of his educational qualifications, for example, if he is an administrative assistant then this could be assessed as a Skill Set 3 or 2 role, regardless of the fact that the employee holds a bachelor's degree.

10.3.   OVERTIME

The Labour Law prohibits employers from requiring young persons to work overtime in any circumstances, remain at the workplace after the prescribed working times or be employed on a rest day.

Adult employees who work overtime shall be paid their full remuneration, plus a supplement of at least 25% of their basic salary, or 50% where the overtime is worked between 10:00 p.m. and 4:00 a.m. Where the overtime is worked during the employee's rest day or on a UAE public holiday, an employer may choose between (i) providing the employee a day's holiday in lieu of the day worked; or (ii) applying a 50% uplift on the employee's basic salary for all hours worked by the employee on the day worked.

Employees may not be required to work more than two hours of overtime per day and no more than 144 hours every three week period.

In the UAE, Friday used to be the normal weekly rest day for all employees; however, this changed following an announcement from the government mandating public sector employees and schools to work Monday to Friday (with Friday being a half-day) from 1 January 2022. Private sector employers are free to choose their working week with many opting for Monday to Friday. The Labour Law prohibits an employee, other than a daily paid employee, from working on more than two successive rest days.

The Labour Law exempts the following categories of employees from receiving an overtime entitlement:

(a) chairperson and members of the board of directors;
(b) persons occupying supervisory positions if such positions would enable them to enjoy the powers of the employer;
(c) crews of naval vessels and other workers at sea;
(d) businesses whose technical nature requires continuation of work through successive shifts or tours (provided that the average working hours do not exceed fifty-six hours per week); and
(e) preparatory or complementary works which must necessarily be carried out outside the time limits generally established for work in the facility.

While the DIFC Employment Law provides that employees may opt out of the maximum working week, it does not provide for statutory overtime rates.

Under the ADGM Employment Regulations a new compensation regime for overtime has been introduced for employees. Employees are entitled to overtime for time worked in excess of 832 hours over a four-month period (the Threshold). Overtime is not to be compensated for employees in a managerial or supervisory position or positions reasonably expected within that industry internationally not to be entitled to overtime.

10.4. MEAL AND REST PERIODS

Employers in the UAE must allow employees to take a rest break for rest, meals and prayer, amounting to not less than one hour in total, after working for five successive hours. Employers are required to give employees one rest day per week. Rest breaks are not included in calculating working hours.

DIFC Employment Law and ADGM Employment Regulations provide for a one-hour rest period in aggregate in a six-hour period.

10.5. DEDUCTIONS FROM WAGES

If there is a shortfall in wage payments made to an employee, he or she can raise a complaint with the MHRE.

The Labour Law prohibits any deductions from an employee's wages, except in the following circumstances:

(a) Recovery of loans granted to the employee, subject to a maximum of 50% of the employee's remuneration;
(b) recovery of advances or money paid to an employee in excess of his or her entitlements (provided such a deduction does not exceed 20% of the employee's remuneration);
(c) any contributions that the employee is legally required to pay from his or her remuneration such as pension contributions;
(d) where the worker contributes to a savings fund;
(e) contributions towards any welfare scheme or in respect of any other privileges or services provided by the employer;
(f) fines imposed upon the employee for any offence he or she has committed (subject to a maximum of 5% of the employee's remuneration);
(g) any debt payable further to a court judgment, provided that the deduction shall not exceed one-quarter of the employee's remuneration; and
(h) such amount as is necessary to repair or replace property damaged or destroyed as a result of the employee's actions or violation of instructions (to a maximum of five days' remuneration per month).

If there are multiple reasons for deductions, the maximum deduction permitted is 50% of the employee's remuneration.

An employee who is not paid for sixty days may consider himself discharged and apply to the MHRE for permission to take up alternative employment and unilaterally transfer his sponsorship for a work permit and residency visa purposes.

Under the DIFC Employment Law and ADGM Employment Regulations, an employer may deduct sums from the employee's remuneration if:

– the deduction or payment is required or authorized under a statutory provision or the employee's employment contract;
– the employee has previously agreed in writing to the deduction or payment;
– the deduction or payment is a reimbursement for an overpayment of wages or expenses; or
– the deduction or payment has been ordered by the applicable court.

10.6.   GARNISHMENT

Attachments to earnings are possible through a court order, and deductions may be made accordingly by an employer.

10.7.   EXEMPTIONS TO WAGE AND HOUR LAWS

The Labour Law exempts the following categories of employees from receiving an overtime entitlement:

(a) chairperson and members of the board of directors;
(b) persons occupying supervisory positions if such positions would enable them to enjoy the powers of the employer;
(c) crews of naval vessels and other workers at sea;
(d) businesses whose technical nature requires continuation of work through successive shifts or tours (provided that the average working hours do not exceed fifty-six hours per week); and
(e) preparatory or complementary works which must necessarily be carried out outside the time limits generally established for work in the facility.

10.8.   CHILD LABOUR

The Labour Law prohibits the employment of anyone younger than 15 years of age. Prior to recruiting a young person over the age of 15 years, an employer must obtain the following documents from the individual:

– a certificate of medical fitness for the required work;
– written consent from the young person's guardian or custodian.

The Labour Law requires employers to maintain a special register of young persons at the workplace, showing each young person's name, age, address, date of recruitment, role and the full name of their guardian. The Labour Law does not define 'young person', but full legal age is generally accepted as being 18 years old.

As of January 2011, Ministerial Resolution No. 1189 of 2010 allows for the issue of Juvenile Work Permits for the employment of minors from 15 to 18 years who hold an existing valid residence in their passport. The Executive Regulations further provide for the ability to obtain Juvenile work permits. Permits may be issued for a period not exceeding one year, and there are restrictions on the type of work and hours of employment. The resolution specifies thirty-one categories of work in which juveniles are not permitted to work, including but not limited to underground jobs in mines, quarries and other industrial work-related to mining; furnaces of melting metals; oil refining; bakeries; asphalt industry, and so on. The Executive Regulations further provide that young persons may not be employed in hazardous or harmful works and industries, or occupations likely to endanger the health or safety of the young person, due to the nature of the occupation or the circumstances under which it is performed.

The DIFC Employment Law and ADGM Employment Regulations contain no specific provisions regarding the employment of minors apart from a provision stating that employees must be at least 15 years of age under the ADGM Employment Regulations and 16 years of age under the DIFC Employment Law.

10.9.   Record-Keeping Requirements

10.9.1.   Information That Must Be Maintained

An employer must maintain information regarding each of its employees for payroll purposes and in order to demonstrate compliance with the Labour Law in the event of labour inspection. Article 13 of the Labour Law requires records to be maintained for a minimum period of two years following termination.

10.9.2.   Records That Must Be Maintained

The Labour Law does not prescribe the records that must be maintained by employers but it would be prudent for employers to maintain the following records:

(1) A personnel file for each employee with the following information: (i) employee name; (ii) job; (iii) age; (iv) nationality; (v) place of residence; (vi) marital status; (vii) date of employment; (viii) wage and any adjustments; (ix) disciplinary sanctions imposed; (x) occupational injuries and diseases sustained; and (xi) date and reason of termination.

(2) A leave card for each employee separately detailing annual leave, sick leave and other leave.

Employers employing GCC nationals should maintain documents evidencing the employee's registration with the State pension authority, both in the UAE and the home country, as well as the contributions made for each year of the employment.

Although there is no strict legal obligation to maintain copies of employment contracts or labour cards, it would be advisable for an employer to do so, as well as to keep copies of employee's passports and residency visas. It is unlawful in the UAE for an employer to retain an employee's passport. Any retention would have to be with employee consent.

Employers who employ fifty or more workers are also required to set rules regarding the organization of work, such as the regulation of work instructions, penalties, promotions and rewards, and the procedures for terminating the employment relationship. Employers employing fifty or more employees are also required to have in place a system for complaints and grievances that employees have access to.

Under the DIFC Employment Law (except for seconded employees) and the ADGM Employment Regulations, an employer must issue payslips to employees, maintain personnel records with all employees' information, and issue employees with written statements of their main terms and conditions of employment. Under the ADGM Employment Regulations, these records should be maintained for two years after the employment terminates and under the DIFC Employment Law, the time frame for maintaining the same is six years after the employment terminates.

10.9.3. Failure to Maintain Required Records

An employer without proper and up-to-date records will not be in a position to defend any claims brought by an employee such as payment in lieu of accrued untaken holiday or unpaid wages.

10.10. REDUCTIONS IN COMPENSATION CAUSED BY ECONOMIC DOWNTURN

Any reduction in compensation must be agreed with an employee as a matter of contract, and an employer does not have the right to unilaterally vary an employee's contractual compensation. Another consideration for an employer is that the end of service gratuity is calculated on an employee's final salary. Therefore, reducing an employee's basic salary has a knock-on effect on this statutory entitlement, and an employee may insist on having his accrued end of service paid out on termination of the existing contract under the higher salary. An employee and employer will need to enter into a new MHRE contract to record the revised compensation, and in some cases, the MHRE has insisted on the employee attending in person to sign the new contract at the Ministry, in order for it to ensure that the employee is freely agreeing to the reduction.

10.11. CHECKLIST OF DO'S AND DON'TS

- Maintain clear payroll records of all payments and deductions made to employees.
- Maintain records in line with the Labour Law in order to demonstrate compliance, should a Labour Inspector request to see such records.
- Pay employees through the WPS, or record details of employees who are not paid through WPS and reasons why.
- Keep records of working hours and overtime.

11. OTHER WORKINGS CONDITIONS AND BENEFITS: BY STATUTE, COLLECTIVE AGREEMENTS OR COMPANY POLICY

11.1. HEALTH AND OTHER INSURANCE

Under the Health Insurance Law for the Emirate of Dubai (No. 11 of 2013) (the Health Insurance Law), health insurance is compulsory for all residents of, and visitors to, the Emirate of Dubai including all the free zones within the Emirate. The obligation to provide health insurance cover for UAE expatriate residents falls to employers and sponsors. In addition to its general impact on employers, residents and visitors to the Emirate, the Health Insurance Law has wide-ranging implications for the health insurance market (principally insurers, Third-Party Administrators (TPAs) and brokers) and healthcare providers. The Health Insurance Law was out in phases between 2014 and 2016 on employers and on the insurance market in Dubai.

The following is a summary of key requirements:

(1) Employers are responsible for the provision of health insurance for their employees, sponsors for their dependants.

(2) The government of Dubai is responsible for UAE nationals resident in Dubai.

(3) Complying with the health insurance requirements is a prerequisite to an individual obtaining a residency or visit visa.

(4) There is mandated minimum coverage, in the form of a basic health plan, which differs for UAE nationals, expats and visitors; it is permissible to provide enhanced cover over and above the mandated essential package.

(5) Insurers, TPAs, brokers and healthcare providers require an annual Dubai Health Authority (DHA) permit in order to carry on their medical business in Dubai.

(6) Only DHA 'Participating Insurers' are permitted to provide the mandated minimum health insurance coverage.

(7) The DHA publishes an approved price list for medical services and healthcare providers required to adhere to the approved pricing.

(8) DHA approval is required to offer insurance plans and for associated premium charges.

In Abu Dhabi, an employer is required to provide medical/health insurance for all employees, as well as the employee's family (which includes spouse and up to three children below the age of 18 years old). The insurance applies from the date of arrival in the UAE and not the date of commencement of employment.

Previously, UAE nationals in Abu Dhabi received free medical insurance and, therefore, there was no obligation on the employer to provide health insurance generally to its UAE national employees. However, an Executive Decision of 2007 changed the position by providing that the Health Insurance Laws apply to all employees who are UAE citizens (i.e., those who hold UAE nationality in accordance with the relevant laws). The cost of the insurance policy (i.e., annual premium) inclusive of any registration fees is payable by the employer. In the event that the employer/sponsor does attempt to pass on the cost of providing health insurance cover to the employee, this would be considered a violation of the Health Insurance Law. However, the employer is entitled to require the employee to pay a 'deductible', which is an amount payable by the employee directly to the medical services provider at the time of the visit.

11.2. PENSION AND RETIREMENT BENEFITS

Conceptually, end of service gratuity is an entitlement designed to be in lieu of a pension provision. Under the previous labour law, in limited circumstances, it was possible to provide that a contributory pension scheme or savings fund will be provided in place of the statutory entitlement to end of service gratuity. However, such provision has not been provided for under the current Labour Law and currently this is not an option for employers.

Under the ADGM Employment Regulations, if an employer wishes to offer a contributory pension fund in place of the end of service gratuity, then it must ask the employee to make the election in writing (which can be made at any time during the employment). Once that election is made, the employee cannot then unilaterally change his mind and opt for the end of service gratuity.

UAE nationals and nationals of GCC Member States are entitled to membership of the State pension fund and to receive contributions from their employers and also the State (rather than receiving an end of service gratuity in accordance with the Labour Law). There are two pensions' authorities in the UAE, one specific to the Emirate of Abu Dhabi and the other being the federal pensions authority.

The contributions are as follows: 5% employee, 12.5% employer and 2.5% from the State under the federal pensions fund scheme; and 5% employee, 15% employer and 6% from the State under the Emirate of Abu Dhabi's pension fund scheme. GCC nationals are entitled to receive and to make contributions according to their home country State schemes. There are also upper earning levels set in each of the GCC country's pension legislation, meaning that an employee whose remuneration exceeds the stated upper earnings level is entitled to end of service gratuity on the excess.

In the DIFC, the DIFC Authority has replaced the previous arrangement of end of service gratuity, payable on termination of employment, with a defined contribution savings scheme, in which contributions are made monthly into a scheme called a Qualifying Scheme. The Qualifying Scheme which is being supported by the DIFC Authority is the DEWS plan; however, employers may choose to use a Qualifying Alternative Scheme or obtain an exemption in relation to another Qualifying Scheme. End of service gratuity ceased to accrue after 31 January 2020 and employers are obliged to make monthly contributions into DEWS or other Qualifying Scheme from 1 February 2020. Employers were given until 30 April 2020 to enrol in the scheme.

11.3. VACATION AND HOLIDAY PAYMENTS ON TERMINATION

Under the Labour Law, an employee is entitled to no fewer than two days of leave for every calendar month if his or her continuous service is more than six months and less than one year. Employees who have more than one year of continuous service are entitled to not fewer than thirty calendar days of annual leave for each year of employment. Employees who work part time will receive a pro-rata entitlement according to the percentage hours worked. Employees in the private sector are also entitled to public holidays, as declared by the Government, of which there are normally ten per year.

The employer can fix the date of commencement of annual leave subject to providing one-month prior notice. In practice, many employers will operate a system whereby employees are permitted to take leave in blocks of a day provided proper advance notice is given.

Parties may agree to carry over accrued unused annual leave to the following leave year up to a maximum of half of the annual leave entitlement or agree to be paid in lieu. The employer cannot prevent the employee from taking annual leave for more than two years without the employee's agreement. Any payment in lieu of accrued unused annual leave on termination of employment is based on the employee's basic salary.

The DIFC Employment Law and ADGM Employment Regulations provide for twenty working days of annual leave (for employees who have accrued ninety days' employment service), and an employer can fix the periods of leave in line with its business needs. Payment in lieu of accrued annual leave is only permitted on termination of employment but may be made under the Labour Law during employment.

An employer may serve a notice of dismissal on an employee while that employee is on leave (whether annual leave, maternity leave or sick leave), but notice will not commence until the employee has returned to work.

11.4. LEAVES OF ABSENCE

11.4.1. Personal Leave

Hajj leave is currently not provided for under the Labour Law.

The ADGM Employment Regulations provide for the same entitlement, whereas the DIFC Employment law provides for twenty-one days Hajj leave, once during the employee's employment, following completion of one year of continuous service. Apart from this entitlement, any personal leave policy or personal days is a matter for an employer to adopt as company policy.

11.4.2. Medical or Sick Leave

An employee who has completed his or her probationary period is entitled to take up to ninety days of sick leave, consecutive or non-consecutive, for each year of service. Such employees are entitled to receive sick pay as follows:

– the first fifteen days with full pay;
– the next thirty days with half pay;
– any subsequent period(s) without pay.

Unpaid sick leave may be granted during the probationary period upon production of a medical certificate.

No sick leave is payable if the employee's illness is a direct result of his or her own misconduct (e.g., consumption of alcohol or drugs).

An employer may terminate the employment of an individual after he or she has exhausted his or her sick leave entitlement if the employee is unable to resume the requirements of the position. During statutory sick leave, an employee may resign from employment and claim the remainder of his or her statutory sick pay in lieu thereof, provided the employee can submit medical evidence showing that his or her resignation is due to his or her medical condition.

The DIFC Employment Law and ADGM Employment Regulations provide for an employee to receive sixty days of sick leave per year (ten days with full pay, twenty days with half pay and remaining thirty days with no pay). There are no restrictions on this entitlement, for example, completion of a probationary period. Once the employee has exhausted sick leave and sick pay entitlement, the employer may terminate employment with immediate effect on written notice to the employee (not applicable under the DIFC Employment Law where sick leave is taken on account of a disability).

11.4.3. Bereavement Leave

Employees are entitled to the following bereavement leave under the Labour Law:

(a) up to a maximum of five days in the case of the death of the employee's spouse; and

(b) up to a maximum of three days in the case of the death of the employee's children, parents, siblings, grandparents, or grandchildren.

Employees are required to submit proof of death once they return to work.

11.4.4. Parental Leave

The Labour Law provides for five working days of parental leave which must be taken within the first six months following the birth of the child. The DIFC Employment Law and the ADGM Employment Regulations do not make any provision for parental leave. The Labour Law, DIFC Employment Law and the ADGM Employment Regulations do not make any provision for emergency leave or time off for caring for dependants. There is also no entitlement to request flexible working. Many international employers will adopt company policies providing for such leave on a limited basis as part of operating integrated international policies for their employees.

11.4.5. Pregnancy and Maternity Leave

A working woman is entitled to forty-five days maternity leave with full pay and fifteen days maternity leave on half pay once she has completed a minimum of six months of pregnancy. In addition, a female employee can take a maximum of forty-five (consecutive or non-consecutive) days' leave, without pay, if she suffers from an illness resulting from pregnancy or birth and, as a result, is unable to resume work. Such illness should be evidenced by a medical certificate issued by a UAE licensed medical practitioner/authority.

Employees are also entitled to take an additional thirty days of paid leave followed by an additional thirty days of unpaid leave following their maternity leave in instances where their baby is affected by a disability or a medical condition which requires full-time care, subject to a medical certificate being provided.

Maternity leave does not count as part of any other leave. This means that a female employee cannot be on both maternity and sick leave concurrently; it must be one or the other.

Furthermore, employers are not permitted to dismiss an employee or serve notice of termination due to the employee's pregnancy or maternity leave.

Under the Labour Law, employees have no entitlement to paternity leave. The DIFC Employment Law and ADGM Employment Regulations entitle male employees to take paternity leave of up to five working days. Under the DIFC Employment Law such entitlement is subject to the employee being employed for twelve continuous months and subject to the employee notifies the employer at least eight weeks prior to the expected date of delivery.

The DIFC Employment Law and the ADGM Employment Regulations provide for an employee who has accrued twelve months of service by the expected week of delivery to receive sixty-five working days of maternity leave. She must also notify her employer of her pregnancy eight weeks before her expected week of delivery (if requested by the employer) and serve twenty-one days of notice of the date on which she wishes to commence maternity leave. She must also provide a medical report confirming the date of excepted delivery. Payment during maternity leave includes thirty-three working days of full pay and thirty-two working days of half pay.

The DIFC Employment Law and the ADGM Employment Regulations also provide that a female employee adopting a child younger than five years under the DIFC Employment Law, and three months under the ADGM Employment Regulations, is entitled to the same leave as a pregnant employee.

11.4.6. Nursing Leave

For six months following the date of delivery, the employee is entitled to a maximum of two breaks a day amounting to a total of one hour to nurse her child, without any loss to remuneration. Such breaks are counted as being part of the employee's hours of work and are paid. This benefit is not replicated in the ADGM Employment Regulations; however, the DIFC Employment Law provides that female employees returning to work are entitled to take a one-hour nursing break where they work in excess of six hours a day for a period of six months following childbirth.

11.4.7.   Injury at Work

The Labour Law provides for workmen's compensation if an employee suffers an injury at work. If the injury is a result of the employee's own negligence, then an employer can refuse to cover medical expenses and pay compensation. Accidents at work and diseases contracted as a result of an employee being exposed in the workplace must be logged and reported to the MHRE and the police which will inspect the workplace, interview employees and produce a report with recommendations. Failure to comply with reporting requirements attracts a fine of AED 10,000 per incident. Where an injury at work occurs, an employer could be faced with administrative fines, criminal liability and civil liability to compensate the employee.

11.5.   ACCOMMODATION

Employers with more than fifty employees are required to provide those employees who are earning less than AED 2,000 a month (pursuant to the Wage Protection System) with free accommodation according to Ministerial Resolution No. 591 of 2016. Such accommodation must meet the standards and criteria already in place for labour accommodation.

   Local authorities are given the power to extend the scope of the resolution to employers with less than fifty employees or to employees earning above the AED 2,000 threshold. Failure to comply may result in penalties being issued by the MHRE.

11.6.   CHECKLIST OF DO'S AND DON'TS

– Have clear company policies regarding family-friendly policies.
– Consider operating best practice policies with regard to paternity, maternity and adoption leave; possibly awarding unpaid leave in the absence of legislative obligations providing for paid leave.
– Ensure that employees are familiar with notification requirements for taking leave (of whatever nature).
– Ensure that health and safety policies and rules are clearly displayed, together with reporting procedures for workplace accidents.

12. WORKERS' COMPENSATION

12.1. OVERVIEW

If an employee sustains an accident at work or contracts an occupational disease, the Labour Law requires the employer to pay for the cost of the employee's treatment in a local government or public medical centre until he or she recovers or is classified as disabled. The treatment for which the employer is responsible extends to the residence in a hospital or sanatorium, surgical operations, X-rays, medical analysis, the purchase of medicines, rehabilitation equipment and the supply of artificial limbs (or other prosthetic appliances) if the employee is declared disabled. The employer is also responsible for meeting the cost of the employee's transport to and from treatment.

The Labour Law also states that if an employee's injury prevents him or her from working, the employer shall pay a cash allowance to the employee equal to his or her full pay throughout the period of treatment, or for six months, whichever is the shorter. If the employee's treatment extends beyond a period of six months, he or she shall be entitled to receive a cash allowance equal to half of his or her pay for an additional six months or until the employee has fully recovered, his disability is confirmed, or he or she dies, whichever occurs first.

The Labour Law states that employees who have sustained an employment accident or contracted an occupational disease that has left them partially or permanently disabled are entitled to receive compensation at a level prescribed by the Labour Law. This amount is payable by the employer and is measured according to the permanent disability suffered (e.g., loss of a thumb or arm). For permanent disability or death, current compensation is set at twenty-four months' remuneration, subject to a minimum of AED 18,000 and a maximum of AED 200,000. If an employee dies as a result of a workplace accident or disease, then an employer may also be liable for 'diya' or blood money to compensate the employee's family (currently around AED 200,000).

The ADGM Employment Regulations provide for compensation to be paid by the employer to the employee in the event of the employee sustaining a work-related injury or disease or dies as a result of a work-related injury or disease. The DIFC Employment Law provides the same entitlement but only where the accident or illness arose as a result of the employer's negligence.

12.2.   CHECKLIST OF DO'S AND DON'TS

– Keep up-to-date logs of any workplace accidents or diseases.
– Maintain insurance cover and ensure that adequate cover is in place.
– Monitor employees who do suffer injury to ensure that they receive adequate medical care and that permanent disability is avoided in so far as possible.

13.   COMPANY'S OBLIGATIONS TO PROVIDE A SAFE AND HEALTHY WORKPLACE

13.1.   OVERVIEW OF SAFETY AND ENVIRONMENTAL LAWS AND REGULATIONS

The Labour Law obliges all employers to put in place rules regulating health and safety in the workplace. These rules must be displayed in a conspicuous place in the workplace. Employees are also under an obligation to maintain health and safety procedures and to comply with their duties so that the employer does not suffer loss and colleagues are not exposed to danger with regard to their health and safety.

13.2.   REQUIREMENTS

An employer should exhibit health and safety procedures in a conspicuous place in the workplace. Such instructions should be in Arabic, and if necessary, translated into a language easily accessible to employees. An employer should also provide minimum facilities and access to medical facilities.

As stated above in section 3.1, construction and industrial sector employers, with a workforce of five hundred or more persons, are now also required to employ an Emirati health and safety officer.

13.3.   RIGHTS OF EMPLOYEES

Employers are also obliged to provide first aid kits and first aiders (one box per each one hundred workers), drinking water and facilities (toilets), as well as any necessary protective equipment and clothing for carrying out the work the employee is engaged to do. Workplaces should be well ventilated and clean with adequate lighting.

If the workforce is in danger of being exposed to certain listed occupational diseases, the employer should provide employees with regular medical examinations.

The MHRE has issued regulations governing the conditions in labour camps, which consist of housing typically provided for construction workers or other manual labourers. These regulations cover issues such as the number of permitted employees who may be asked to share washing facilities, kitchens and rooms, as well as the provision of leisure facilities.

As stated above in section 11.5, Ministerial Resolution No. 591 of 2016 obliges employers with over fifty employees to provide accommodation to such employees who earn a gross monthly wage of less than AED 2,000.

MHRE may propose an increase or decrease in the daily working hours for certain sectors or certain categories of workers as well as specify the work timings and breaks and the hours during which working shall be prohibited for certain categories of workers.

In the Emirate of Abu Dhabi and Dubai, it is obligatory to provide employees with medical insurance. The Labour Law also required employers to provide medical aid specialists to provide first aid and supply a first aid kit.

13.4.   RIGHTS OF EMPLOYER

If an employee fails to follow health and safety procedures, then an employer is not liable for the injury suffered by an employee. Further, loss caused to the employer by an employee can be recovered from the employee's wages and deducted at a rate of five working days' wages. An employee can also be dismissed without notice if he commits an act of negligence causing substantial loss to his employer, provided an employer notifies the MHRE of the incident within forty-eight hours of the incident taking place, or if he violates health and safety procedures.

13.5.   SPECIFIC STANDARDS

The specific requirements are set out above.

13.6.   INJURY OR ACCIDENT AT WORK

Accidents or injuries suffered at work must be logged in an accident book, and an employer has to cover the cost for an employee to receive medical treatment and continue paying the employee his salary for a specific period of time. Depending on the seriousness of the accident, it may need to be reported to the MHRE and the police.

13.7. WORKPLACE VIOLENCE

An employer can dismiss an employee for workplace violence or an assault on a colleague without notice. The employee could also be subject to a police complaint.

13.8. FINES AND PENALTIES

Breach of health and safety would be a breach of the Labour Law, and a labour inspector could impose a fine of between AED 5,000 and AED 1,000,000. The MHRE is tasked with inspecting labour accommodation and may impose a fine for failure to comply with a notification identifying shortcomings and ordering corrections to be made.

13.9. CHECKLIST DO'S AND DON'TS

– Display health and safety procedures in a conspicuous place for all employees to view, in a language accessible to employees.
– Make employees aware of their obligations and the consequences of not following proper procedures.
– Ensure up-to-date and correct records are maintained.
– Ensure proper insurance cover for workplace accidents is taken out.
– Ensure proper health insurance cover is taken out.

14. IMMIGRATION, SECONDMENT AND FOREIGN ASSIGNMENT

14.1. OVERVIEW LAWS CONTROLLING IMMIGRATION

A key feature of the workforce in the UAE is its expatriate nature, with almost 90% of the labour force consisting of non-UAE nationals. This characteristic means that immigration regulations are a key consideration for all employers; with the main piece of legislation being Law No. 29 of 2021 (together with the implementing regulations) and numerous Ministerial Resolutions (Immigration Law).

Every employee who is not a UAE national (or a national of an Arabian GCC Member State) must be sponsored for a work permit and residency purposes by a UAE-based employing entity in order to work lawfully in the UAE. Sponsorship regulations are a significant factor in employment relations given the small size of the UAE national working-age population and the consequent requirement for foreign labour at all levels of the workforce. The sponsorship system is used to regulate and monitor the number of foreign nationals in the UAE, and those not sponsored by an employer (whether directly or indirectly as the dependant of a sponsored employee) are unable to remain for long periods of time in the UAE. Sponsorship for work purposes is usually conditional on employees being at least 18 years of age (subject to exceptions discussed in section 10.8) and not more than 65. Sponsorship for those between the age of 65 and 70 years is assessed on a case-by-case basis and usually is granted only if the individual has specialist skills and experience.

14.2.   RECRUITING, SCREENING AND HIRING PROCESS

Integral elements of the sponsorship process are for the individual to be required to produce his or her educational certificates attested and authenticated by the UAE embassy in the country of issue, and by the Ministry of Foreign Affairs and International Cooperation in the UAE; the individual must also undergo a blood test once he or she has entered the UAE showing that he or she is free of contagious diseases (in particular HIV and hepatitis B and C); the employer must give a bank guarantee (meant to cover the costs of repatriation) to the MHRE (or the free zone authority), and an offer letter and employment contract in a prescribed form must be registered with the MHRE or the free zone authority. Certain nationalities may be required by the MHRE to complete medical tests prior to entry into the UAE. Such individuals would still have to undergo medical tests once in the UAE.

Organizations are grouped into categories, pursuant to the extent of their compliance with legislation, legal regulations and standards, which then determine the amount of fees they pay and the bank guarantee required upon recruitment. Where the employer is in a free zone, these requirements apply in relation to the relevant free zone authority and not the MHRE or the Immigration Department. Under arrangements in the free zones, the free zone authority itself and not the employer will act as the sponsor, thus reducing the administrative burden on businesses within the free zone. However, each employing entity must enter into a personnel sponsorship agreement in a prescribed form under which any and all liability arising out of the employment will be taken on by the employing entity.

14.3.   THE OBLIGATION OF EMPLOYER TO ENFORCE IMMIGRATION LAWS

An employer is under a duty to ensure that every employee working for it is properly sponsored for a work permit and residency visa purposes. The employer should also ensure that an employee does not work for a third party without specific consent for the arrangement from the relevant UAE authorities.

14.4.   FINES AND PENALTIES

Employing an employee unlawfully attracts a fine under the Labour Law of between AED 50,000 and AED 200,000 (which is multiplied by the number of employees in respect to whom the violation occurred up to a maximum of AED 10,000,000), and a fine of AED 50,000 under the Immigration Law. The employer's classification would also be automatically downgraded by the MHRE. There are also foreign ownership restrictions in the UAE outside of the free zones for certain types of companies (in which 100% foreign ownership of companies is permitted). For certain types of companies, if a foreign business wishes to set up a limited liability company 'onshore', then it must partner with a UAE National or UAE company which will hold 51% of the shares in the entity. A key point of any entity established outside of a free zone in 'onshore' or 'mainland' Dubai or the UAE is that the MHRE will have jurisdiction and the employing entity must be registered with it. The name of the UAE partner, where applicable, will be registered with the MHRE and if any issue is identified by the MHRE leading it to block one entity's ability to apply for or renew work permits and residency visas or make any application to the MHRE, all entities registered under the UAE partner's name will also be blocked. Foreign ownership restrictions have significantly been relaxed in the last year.

14.5.   SECONDMENT/FOREIGN ASSIGNMENT

International secondments are not formally recognized by the UAE authorities, and an employee will always be taken to be the employee of his or her UAE sponsor for work permit and residency visa purposes. The UAE sponsor is liable for employee entitlements, and the main entitlements are to minimum notice and to end of service gratuity. An employee on secondment or international assignment from one entity to another, for example, from an employer's London office to its Dubai office, will for all intents and purposes in the UAE be an employee of the Dubai office and covered by the Labour

Law (or the ADGM Employment Regulations if applicable. The position under the DIFC Employment Law differs slightly in that employees on a 'secondment' status can be subject to a different law, except that certain provisions of the DIFC Employment Law will still be applicable to such employment relationship). When the secondment or assignment is completed, the employee will be entitled to end of service gratuity because the employment in the UAE is terminating, even if the employee is moving to another assignment within the corporate group.

Within the UAE, secondment from one entity to another is also restricted, given that under the immigration regulations, an employee is only permitted to work for his or her sponsor/employer. Specific permission from the MHRE must be applied for and obtained, in order for an employee to be seconded from one entity to another. Such permission may be given on a part-time basis so that the employee can continue working for both the third party and his employer or on a full-time basis. If granted, such permission is granted for six months and is renewable.

14.6.   CHECKLIST OF DO'S AND DON'TS

– Ensure that all employees are properly sponsored for work permit and residency visa purposes (with an appropriate visa for the work being carried out).
– Ensure that employment contracts accurately reflect the employment relationship and secondment arrangement.
– Ensure employee liabilities such as the end of service gratuity are accrued for even with regard to international secondees or assignees.

15.   RESTRICTIVE COVENANTS AND PROTECTION OF TRADE SECRETS AND CONFIDENTIAL INFORMATION

15.1.   OVERVIEW

The Labour Law provides that an employer may summarily dismiss an employee who reveals any of the employer's secrets. It also provides that when an employee's employment gives him or her access to the employer's confidential information or trade secrets, the employer may impose post-termination restrictions, provided such restrictions are reasonable in scope, geographical limitation and duration.

Prior to January 2011, upon cancellation of an employee's work permit and residency visa, following termination of employment, the MHRE imposed a mandatory six-month ban on the individual from taking up alternative employment within the UAE. This employment ban could be waived on the satisfaction of specific conditions, including the previous employer's consent unless the employee had accrued three years' service.

In December 2010, Cabinet Decision No. 25 of 2010 was issued on the basis of which the MHRE issued various Executive Ministerial Decisions. This legislation did not abolish the six-month employment ban but regularized the rules under which it could be waived or disapplied. However, in October 2015, the MHRE issued Ministerial Decree No. 766 of 2015 which took effect from 1 January 2016. This decree introduced some key changes in relation to the granting of work permits on the termination of employment, including: (i) employees were able to obtain a new work permit without a twelve-month labour ban being imposed, provided they had complied with their contractual and legal obligations regarding their previous employment; (ii) most unskilled employees continued to require a minimum of six months' service to avoid a labour ban (as opposed to the previous position of two years' service); and (iii) no minimum service requirement for skilled employees to satisfy in order to avoid a labour ban.

The position changed again in February 2022 on implementation of the new Labour Law. Article 9 of the Labour Law provides that, subject to certain exemptions, where a foreign national employee leaves the UAE without complying with the notice requirements during the probationary period, such employee may not be granted a work permit for a period of one year from leaving the country. Likewise, on completion of the probationary period, subject to certain exemptions, where an employee terminates the employment prior to its expiry for an illegal reason, a work permit may not be granted for a period of one year from termination. In such instances, the employer must notify MHRE.

The twelve-month employment ban does not apply to employees who are sponsored and work within a free zone. However, in such cases, if the employee wishes to take up employment with another organization within the same free zone, his or her former employer may request that the free zone authority impose a ban that would preclude the former employee from working for another entity in the free zone. There are no guarantees, however, that the free zone authority will accede to such a request and it would usually require strong evidence of wrongdoing by the employee in question.

In rare cases, an employer can apply to the Immigration Department for a ban on the employee remaining in the UAE on any status whatsoever. Such a ban can only be imposed following a specific application requiring the employer to show that the employee has committed serious wrongdoing (i.e., criminal act) or that he poses a public security risk. Such a ban must be applied for before the sponsorship is cancelled. The MHRE has no jurisdiction within the free zones. However, the immigration department (which does have jurisdiction across the UAE) has in the past stated that if an employment ban is imposed by the MHRE, then it will apply this ban within the free zones so that consistency is achieved. However, in practice, these bans have not largely been applied within the free zones, with the exception of the Dubai Multi-Commodities Centre Free Zone.

Often the most effective way to enforce a post-termination restriction is to provide for garden leave during an employee's notice period. Using such a clause enables the employer to keep the employee out of the workplace but still monitor his actions and restrict the employee's access to sensitive commercial information.

15.2.   The Law of Trade Secrets

The Labour Law and the UAE Civil Code both recognize that an employer's trade secrets and confidential information should be protected and an employee should maintain the confidentiality of the information he gains or has access to as a result of his employment.

Further, Article 432 of the UAE Crimes and Penalties Law (Penal Code) makes it an offence for an individual to use another's confidential information for gain without consent, where such information was obtained in the course of practising his art, craft or profession. The offence is punishable by a fine of AED 20,000 and/or imprisonment of a minimum of one year.

Within the DIFC, the DIFC Law of Obligations 2005 provides that an employee will be in the position of a fiduciary towards his employer, though the extent of his obligations will depend on the employee's role and status and position of trust within the employer's organization.

15.3.   Restrictive Covenants and Non-compete Agreements

Employers will often include post-termination restrictions in contracts of employment such as a restriction on working for a competitor, soliciting or dealing with clients, suppliers, customers, or poaching key employees. However, historically it has proven very difficult to enforce such restrictions in the UAE, as the UAE courts will not grant injunctions, that is, issue an order prohibiting an employee from taking certain action, such as contacting clients, the breach of which would amount to contempt of court by the employee.

Therefore, employers are restricted from claiming damages sustained as a result of the breach. Evidencing such damages can be problematic since the employer has to show actual loss of business as a result of the employee's breach of the restrictions. On this basis, employers in the UAE are normally advised to include a liquidated damages clause in their employment contracts. UAE courts have, in the past, recognized such clauses and subsequently awarded damages to the employer. The liquidated damages must represent a proper assessment of the loss or potential damage the employee would cause the employer and not be exorbitant, so as to work as a penalty for or sanction against the employee moving jobs.

In 2016 MHRE issued Ministerial Resolution No. 297 of 2016 which came into effect on 1 April 2016. This resolution provides that where a final court decision is awarded stating that an employee is bound by a contractual agreement not to compete with its employer, the MHRE is entitled to refuse to grant a new work permit, or revoke an existing work permit issued to such individual for the duration of the non-compete restriction. However, the effects of this resolution have not been seen in practice.

Within the DIFC and ADGM, the injunctive relief is recognized and, therefore, in theory at least an employer could apply to the relevant court for an injunction and if granted, this judgment could be registered within the wider UAE or other jurisdictions. There has, however, to date not been any case law on this issue and it is unclear whether a Dubai Court or a court within the UAE federal court system would recognize and enforce an injunction in the employment context. In order to be enforceable, the post-termination restrictions must be reasonable in terms of scope and duration, going no further than necessary to protect the employer's legitimate business interests. It is also important to note that the restrictions must be reasonable at the time the employee is required to enter into them.

15.4.   CHECKLIST OF DO'S AND DON'TS

– Consider including post-termination restrictions in employment contracts for senior employees.
– Include liquidated damages so long as these provide for potential loss likely to be suffered.
– Put in place confidentiality agreements and monitor access to confidential information by employees.
– Limit access to confidential information on a 'need to know' basis if possible.
– Provide password security on certain documents, divide key documents into sections which makes no sense separately.
– Use garden leave where possible.
– Monitor employees' activities, in particular, once an employee has resigned.

16.   PROTECTION OF WHISTLEBLOWING CLAIMS

16.1.   OVERVIEW

There is no legislation providing for the protection of employees who raise concerns, whether internally or externally, regarding the employer's legal obligations. However, there is increasing consideration being given to this area, especially with regard to listed companies and government-owned entities, whose employees can be regarded as falling under the banner of being public officials; thereby subject to higher codes of conduct and specific penal provisions regarding anti-corruption. It is, therefore, expected that specific legislation would be introduced in the future.

Dubai passed Dubai Law No. 4 of 2016 on Financial Crimes (the Financial Crime Law), which for the first time includes protections for those that report crimes to the newly established Dubai Centre for Economic Security. Article 19 of the Financial Crime Law provides for 'protection for the reporter'. The law stipulates that the reporter's freedom, security and protection shall be guaranteed and that no legal or disciplinary action may be taken against the reporter unless the report is false. However, what is unclear is whether whistleblowing is only protected if it is made to the Centre or to other bodies and will protection extend to reports of crimes elsewhere in the UAE. Furthermore, the Centre has not yet been set up, and therefore, at this stage, the practical implications and application of this new law remain to be seen. International companies are likely to have global codes of conduct and whistleblowing policies and even internal hotlines for employees to raise issues of concern. Obligations under the US foreign corrupt practices Act, Sarbanes-Oxley, and the UK Bribery Act would all necessitate a global approach to whistleblowing.

16.2.   CHECKLIST OF DO'S AND DON'TS

– Have a global policy and code of conduct to ensure consistency.
– Ensure application is consistent and provide staff training.
– Consider having a hotline for employees to raise concerns internally and anonymously.

17. PROHIBITION OF DISCRIMINATION IN THE WORKPLACE

17.1. OVERVIEW OF ANTI-DISCRIMINATION LAWS

The Labour Law prohibits discrimination based on race, colour, sex, religion, national origin, social origin, or because of disability. The Labour Law further provides pursuant to Article 4(4) of the Labour Law that female employees are entitled to receive the same wage as their male counterparts where they are performing the same work or different work of equal value.

Law No. 2 of 2015 on combating discrimination and hatred, as amended also creates a number of criminal offences against discrimination and hatred, and in particular religious hatred which may have potential consequences in an employment context.

The DIFC Employment Law prohibits discrimination between employer and employees on the basis of sex; marital status; race; nationality, religion, age, pregnancy and maternity; mental or physical disability. Discrimination is defined as '(a) where an employee is treated less favourably than others would be treated in the same circumstances on one of the prohibited grounds [...]; (b) in respect of the application of the same provision criterion or practice an employee is put at a disadvantage not faced by others who are not of that sex, marital status, race, nationality, or religion, or suffering from a mental or physical disability, as applicable; or (c) on grounds of one of the prohibited grounds [...], an employee is subjected to unwanted treatment or conduct which has the purpose or effect of creating an intimidating, hostile, degrading, humiliating, or offensive workplace'.

The ADGM Employment Regulations prohibit discrimination between employer and employees on the basis of sex, colour, marital status, race, nationality, or religion, age or disability. Discrimination is defined as '(a) an Employee is treated less favourably than others would be treated in the same circumstances on one of the prohibited grounds [...]; (b) in respect of the application of the same provision, criterion, or practice, an Employee is put at a disadvantage not faced by others who are not of that sex, marital status, race, nationality, religion or age, or suffering from a disability as applicable; or (c) on grounds of one of the prohibited grounds [...], an Employee is subjected to unwanted treatment or conduct which has the purpose or effect of creating an intimidating, hostile, degrading, humiliating or offensive workplace'.

The DIFC Employment Law and the ADGM Employment Regulations make it unlawful for an employer to refuse to continue to employ, or to discriminate regarding employment or any term or condition of employment on the basis of the employee being a member of one of the protected classes set out above. They do permit discrimination based on genuine occupational requirement (save that under the ADGM Employment Regulations, it must be a bona fide occupational requirement which is 'reasonably necessary for the normal performance of a particular role or occupation'). The DIFC Employment Law also introduces a defence to a direct age discrimination claim if an employer can show objective justification. With respect to a provision, criteria or practice, this is where an apparently neutral requirement applies to all, but has the effect of placing those in a protected class at a disadvantage, as the provision, criteria and practice must be shown to be a proportionate means of achieving a legitimate aim. The DIFC Employment Law, however, provides for further grounds which must be taken into consideration when deciding whether or not discrimination has taken place, such as the perception of the Employee, circumstances of the case and whether it is reasonable for the conduct to have that effect.

The DIFC Employment Law and the ADGM Employment Regulations, therefore, prohibit direct and indirect discrimination as well as harassment by reason of an individual being within a protected class. These provisions are largely untested and, therefore, the scope of the provisions is as yet unclear. The DIFC and ADGM are intended to be common law jurisdictions with the laws being modelled on English law. It is, therefore, expected that when interpreting the provisions, the courts would have regard to English case law in this area.

The ADGM Employment Regulations prohibit discrimination on certain grounds but do not specify an employee's remedy (whether compensatory or otherwise, for example, declarations or recommendations to an employer regarding its work practices). However, it is possible that a discrimination claim could be based on a breach of contract claim, and an employee could argue for loss of earnings suffered as a result of the discriminatory act. It is also possible that an act of discrimination could be regarded as a statutory tort, attracting compensation or 'injury to feelings' compensation.

The DIFC Employment Law compensation is set out above in section 5.3.

17.2.   AGE DISCRIMINATION

Refer to section 17.1 above. There is no statutory retirement age applicable in the private sector in the UAE. However, an employee over 65 can face difficulties in obtaining sponsorship for work permit and residency visa purposes. Sponsorship for those between 65 and 70 is granted on an exceptional basis, and usually for one year (which permit is renewable). GCC nationals are entitled to draw down a State pension at the age of 60 for men and 55 for women.

17.3.   RACE DISCRIMINATION

Refer to section 17.1 above. The Labour Law, the DIFC Employment Law and the ADGM Employment Regulations expressly provide for non-discrimination on the basis of race.

17.4.   SEX DISCRIMINATION/SEXUAL HARASSMENT

Refer to section 17.1 above. The Labour Law further prohibits sexual harassment, bullying, or any verbal, physical or psychological violence against employees by the employer, superiors, colleagues or those working with the employee.

The Penal Code provides that it is a criminal offence to 'obstruct a female in such a manner as to violate her honour by word or deed'. Further, sexual harassment is a criminal offence under the Penal Code. In such circumstances, the employee would need to make a formal complaint to the police. The police are obliged to follow up on any criminal complaint. If the police believe a complaint is groundless, they can dismiss it out of hand. If, however, the police believe a complaint bears further investigation, the matter may be referred to the Public Prosecutor's Office. The matter will then be investigated and, if the Public Prosecutor determines that there is a case to answer, the matter is then referred to the criminal courts.

17.5.   HANDICAP AND DISABILITY DISCRIMINATION

Refer to section 17.1 above. In the event of total disability, Article 42 of the Labour Law provides that the employment contract will come to an end.

Under the DIFC Employment Law, an employer must not discriminate between employees on the basis of an individuals' disability, meaning a physical or mental condition lasting or likely to last for twelve months or more. An employer is also under a duty to make reasonable adjustments to any physical feature of the workplace or applicable provision, criteria or practices that would, if made, enable the employee to otherwise meet the genuine occupational requirement.

Under the ADGM Employment Regulations, 'an employer discriminates against an employee with a disability if a physical feature of the workplace or an applicable provision, criterion or practice puts the disabled employee at a substantial disadvantage in relation to a relevant matter in comparison with persons who are not disabled, and the employer fails to take such steps as it is reasonable to have to take to avoid the disadvantage.'

17.6.   NATIONAL ORIGIN DISCRIMINATION

The Labour Law, the DIFC Employment Law, and the ADGM Employment Regulations provide for nationality and race to be protected classes.

17.7.   RELIGIOUS DISCRIMINATION

It should always be kept in mind that the UAE is an Islamic country and, while the UAE in general is considered to be one of the more liberal countries in the region, statements or acts that are deemed to be anti-Islamic could result in criminal complaints being made. It is a criminal offence to dishonour Islam or to eat or drink in public during the month of Ramadan. Federal Law No. 2 of 2015 on Preventing Discrimination and Hatred also aims at combating religious contempt or intolerance (with a particular emphasis on preventing extremism) and introduces a definition of discrimination. Pursuant to this law, discrimination is prohibited in the context of the incitement, facilitation or act of religious contempt or other intolerance, but also as a stand-alone punishment.

The Labour Law, the DIFC Employment Law, and the ADGM Employment Regulations provide that an employee should not be discriminated against on the basis of his religion.

17.8.   MILITARY STATUS DISCRIMINATION

There are no provisions under the Labour Law, the DIFC Employment Law and the ADGM Employment Regulations prohibiting discrimination on the basis of military status. The UAE introduced compulsory military service in September 2014, and national service is now mandatory for all male UAE nationals who are:

– between 18 and 30 years old;
– medically fit; and
– obtain approval of the National and Reserve Service Committee.

At present service is optional for women. The only son of a family, as well as individuals who are deemed to be medically unfit, will receive a permanent exemption from military service. There are a number of temporary exemptions in respect of those who are the sole providers for their families and also for those serving jail terms.

National service can also be postponed in certain circumstances, for example, where an individual is a student of a university, college, institution and training centre who is less than 29 years old and is enrolled in a course with a duration of two years or more.

Recruits who have completed their General Certificate of Secondary Education will be required to serve nine months, while those who have not will serve two years. Women who volunteer will serve nine months, regardless of their education level.

Private-sector employers will be required to keep the UAE national's role open for him to return to (although temporary cover may be engaged) and continue to pay the employee's salary (although employers may be able to claim a portion of the salary from the UAE Armed Forces). A recruit's job will have to be reserved until they complete their national service, and they will continue to receive their salary, bonus, allowances, promotions and/or raises as if they were performing their job duties.

Further regulations will be introduced to regulate reservists and their release for ongoing training and military exercises.

17.9. PREGNANCY DISCRIMINATION

The Labour Law prohibits employers from terminating or serving a notice of termination to pregnant female employees by reason of their pregnancy or maternity leave.

The DIFC Employment Law and the ADGM Employment Regulations provide that an employer should not discriminate against a pregnant woman (and a woman on maternity under the DIFC Employment Law only), and provides for her right to return to work following maternity leave.

17.10. MARITAL STATUS DISCRIMINATION

Only the DIFC Employment Law and the ADGM Employment Regulations provide for non-discrimination on the basis of marital status; however, the Labour Law prohibits discrimination on the basis of sex.

17.11. SEXUAL ORIENTATION DISCRIMINATION

Sexual orientation is not a protected class under the Labour Law, the DIFC Employment Law, or the ADGM Employment Regulations.

17.12. RETALIATION

The Labour Law prohibits sexual harassment, bullying, or any verbal, physical or psychological violence against employees by the employer, superiors, colleagues or those working with the employee. There is also a provision in the Labour Law providing that if an employee raises a complaint to the MHRE and is then terminated by reason of having raised the claim, then such termination will be an arbitrary dismissal. There is no provision in the ADGM Employment Regulations providing for employees to be protected from victimization if an employee raises a claim of discrimination. The DIFC Employment Law also expressly prohibits the victimization of the employee by the employer and provides for four protected acts under which victimization is prohibited, each of which is connected to proceedings brought under Part 9 (Non-Discrimination) of the law, such as bringing proceedings, giving evidence, making an allegation.

17.13. CONSTRUCTIVE DISCHARGE

It is extremely difficult to argue constructive discharge under the Labour Law. Article 45 of the Labour Law provides that an employee may resign without notice if the employer breaches an express term of his contract, or has assaulted or subjected the employee to violence or harassment during the employee's employment.

It may be possible for an employee in the DIFC to argue that under the Law of Obligations 2005, he can treat himself as being constructively discharged due to a breach of an implied term of mutual trust and confidence. In ADGM, the explicit recognition of common law principles may potentially open the door to employee claims for damages under the common law concept of an implied duty of trust and confidence. However, it is yet to be seen how this may be interpreted and applied in practice.

17.14. CHECKLIST OF DO'S AND DON'TS

– Adopt an equal opportunities policy to achieve an integrated workforce.
– Consider whether any employees on secondment or assignment are covered by discrimination legislation in their home country.
– Assess the impact of any recruitment or other policies on employees and their potential membership of protected classes.

18.   SMOKING IN THE WORKPLACE

18.1.   OVERVIEW

Smoking in workplaces is prohibited in UAE.

18.2.   CHECKLIST OF DO'S AND DON'TS

– Notify all employees of the prohibition on smoking.
– Monitor employees' smoking breaks in order to minimize them.

19.   USE OF DRUGS AND ALCOHOL IN THE WORKPLACE

19.1.   OVERVIEW

Generally, the Labour Law, the DIFC Employment Law and the ADGM Employment Regulations provide that an employee's off duty conduct should not be taken into account in the workplace unless it has an impact on the employee's work or performance.

Strictly speaking, an individual must have an alcohol license in order to buy and consume alcohol in the UAE. The sale of alcohol is restricted to hotels and limited licensed alcohol stores.

The UAE has a zero tolerance to drug use and any employee using unlawful drugs would be committing an offence which the employer could be under a duty to report to the police. Under the UAE Penal Code, knowing a crime has been committed and failing to report it is in itself an offence.

The commission of a criminal offence or the arrest of an employee under suspicion would entitle the employer to suspend the employee without pay until such criminal investigation or prosecution is completed and the outcome known. The employee could then be reinstated – or terminated – depending on the outcome of such proceedings.

The Labour Law permits an employer to terminate an employee without notice or the payment of end of service gratuity if he is under the influence of drugs or alcohol at work.

19.2.   CHECKLIST OF DO'S AND DON'TS

– Notify all employees of a zero tolerance to drugs and alcohol.
– Ensure the disciplinary policy makes it clear that the use of alcohol or drugs will be a disciplinary offence possibly resulting in termination.

20. AIDS, HIV, SARS, BLOOD-BORNE PATHOGENS

20.1. OVERVIEW

As stated in section 3.5, as part of the sponsorship application process, an employee is required to undergo a medical examination, including a blood test for contagious diseases which will include HIV and Hepatitis (strands B and C) and an X-ray testing for TB. Women may also be tested for pregnancy. If an employee tests positive for infectious diseases, he or she would be required to leave the UAE. Certain nationalities may be required to complete medical tests prior to entry into the UAE as well as undergo medical tests once in the UAE.

20.2. CHECKLIST OF DO'S AND DON'TS

– Ensure employees are aware of the requirement for a medical examination as part of the sponsorship application and renewal process.

21. DRESS AND GROOMING REQUIREMENTS

21.1. OVERVIEW

It is commonplace for employers to have dress codes which require employees to conform to standard dress codes, for example, to require male employees to wear suits, trim beards, wear ties. However, it is also true to say that particularly during the summer months, strict dress codes are relaxed or modified.

Many emirates in UAE also have public codes of conduct (e.g., both Dubai and Sharjah have such policies) providing for dress codes in public requiring both men and women to dress modestly, meaning shoulders, chest and legs must be covered. It is not uncommon to see signs in public shopping malls instructing individuals to maintain proper codes of dress.

21.2. CHECKLIST OF DO'S AND DON'TS

– Maintain a company dress policy and ensure employees are familiar with it.
– Remind employees regularly of the policy and particularly during certain periods of the year, for example, at the beginning of Ramadan.

22. PRIVACY, TECHNOLOGY AND TRANSFER OF PERSONAL DATA

22.1. PRIVACY RIGHTS OF EMPLOYEES

Federal Decree Law No. 45 of 2021 on the Protection of Personal Data (DPL) came into effect from 2 January 2022 and comprehensively regulates the storing and processing of personal data in the UAE. The DPL will not be enforced until six months after the publication of the executive regulations to the DPL has not yet been issued. The DPL restricts the way personal data can be collected, processed, reviewed, and transferred by organizations and investigators in the UAE (excluding DIFC and ADGM). As with the DIFC and ADGM data protection laws, employee monitoring is permitted so long as notice is given to the employee and the employee consents. However, personal data can be collected, stored and processed only for a specified purpose and for a limited time. The UAE Constitution contains a general right to privacy for individuals, and the use or disclosure of another's personal information may amount to a criminal offence.

The DIFC has data protection legislation in the form of DIFC Law No. 1 of 2007 (as amended by Law No. 1 of 2018), and ADGM has in force the Data Protection Regulations 2021 (which will repeal the Data Protection Regulations 2015 in August 2021 for new ADGM establishments and February 2022 for existing ADGM establishments as at the date the Regulations are published). Both sets of legislation set out the conditions under which an employer can hold and use employees' personal data (defined as any information relating to an identifiable natural person).

An employer should ensure that any personal data is:

– processed fairly, lawfully and securely;
– processed for specified, explicit and legitimate purposes;
– adequate, relevant and not excessive in relation to the purposes for which it is collected and or further processed;
– accurate and where necessary kept up-to-date; and
– kept in a form identifying the subject of the personal data only for as long as it is necessary for the purposes the data was collected.

Personal data can only be processed if:

– the employer holding and processing personal data has obtained the employee's written consent;
– the processing of the personal data is necessary for the performance of a contract to which the employee is a party or in order to take steps at the request of the employee prior to entering into a contract;

- the processing is necessary for complying with a legal obligation to which the employer is subject;
- processing is necessary to protect the vital interests of the employee;
- processing is necessary for the legitimate interests pursued by the employer or a third party to which the data is released except where the employee's compelling legitimate interests override those interests. An employee has the right to know before his or her personal data is sent to a third party.

This legislation also contains provisions providing for enhanced protection where personal sensitive data is processed. Personal sensitive data is personal data revealing or concerning (directly or indirectly) racial or ethnic origin, communal origin, political affiliations or opinions, religious or philosophical beliefs, criminal record, and health or sex life.

The employee's rights under this legislation are to:

- object to the processing;
- request that any inaccuracies are rectified;
- request and obtain details of the personal data being held, the purpose for its processing, the source of the data and to whom it has been disclosed;
- make a complaint to the Commissioner of Data Protection who has responsibility for enforcing the data protection legislation in the DIFC or the Data Protection ADGM Registrar; and
- claim damages for loss suffered as a result of contravention of the data protection legislation.

22.2.   CHECKLIST OF DO'S AND DON'TS

- Ensure that any information stored is processed in accordance with legislation.
- Inform employees what information is stored and how it is retained and for how long.
- Permit employees to have access to their information in order for them to correct any errors or query any information held.

23.   WORKPLACE INVESTIGATIONS FOR COMPLAINTS OF DISCRIMINATION, HARASSMENT, FRAUD, THEFT AND WHISTLEBLOWING

23.1.   OVERVIEW

Every employer should have a written disciplinary policy also setting out how investigations will be handled. Under the Labour Law, there is a time limit that an investigation must be initiated within thirty days of the potential disciplinary action. Once an investigation is completed, a disciplinary sanction must be imposed within sixty days.

The Labour Law prohibits sexual harassment, bullying, or any verbal, physical or psychological violence against employees by the employer, superiors, colleagues or those working with the employee.

With respect to fraud and harassment, these would involve police complaints, and an employer could choose to suspend employees without pay pending completion of the criminal process.

An employer must be careful to ensure that all relevant documentation is preserved and be mindful of the general duty to report an offence under the UAE Penal Code.

23.2.   CHECKLIST OF DO'S AND DON'TS

– Follow the company's internal disciplinary and investigation policy.
– Provide for the two processes to be dealt with separately; with different managers carrying out the investigation to those dealing with the disciplinary process.
– Adhere to time limitations when carrying out investigations and disciplinary procedures.

24.   AFFIRMATIVE ACTION/NON-DISCRIMINATION REQUIREMENTS

24.1.   OVERVIEW

The UAE government has sought to encourage the employment of UAE nationals in the private sector by applying a general duty on employers to employ UAE nationals in preference to other nationalities and applying industry-specific quotas as well as the implementation of the Tawteen programme, as stated in section 3.1 above. The banking sector is subject to a requirement to employ 4% of its workforce from UAE nationals, insurance is subject to a 5% quota, and retail or trade is subject to a 2% quota.

Certain specified roles must also be filled by UAE nationals as further detailed in section 3.1 above.

As detailed in section 3.2 above, the Emiratisation Decree (Decree No. 212 of 2018) sets out requirements relating to the recruitment, ongoing support and termination of UAE nationals in the private sector. This resolution repeals Ministerial Resolution No. 176 of 2009, which imposed restrictions on termination of UAE nationals employed in the private sector and Ministerial Resolution No. 293 of 2015 which set out the rules and procedures pertaining to the recruitment of UAE nationals.

Ministerial Resolution No. 212 of 2018

Recruitment

Recruitment requirements are discussed in section 3.2 above.

Ongoing Support

The Emiratisation Decree provides for the MHRE to set up a dedicated unit, which will monitor the employment of UAE nationals, ensure the working environment is appropriate, ensure adequate equipment and resources are provided to the employee, and the employee continues to properly register for social security benefits. It also provides for the MHRE to take a potentially more active role in resolving any workplace disputes as it requires it to have in place a complaints procedure.

Terminations

Various rules and procedures pertaining to termination of UAE nationals apply, including the basis on which such employees may have their employment relationship terminated, what is expected from both employers and employees and the potential consequences for breaching such obligations. Where the contract terminates or expires, employers are expected to undertake an exit interview with the employee.

According to the Emiratisation Decree, UAE nationals may be terminated in any of the following circumstances:

– where a fixed-term contract has expired and has not been renewed;
– by parties' mutual agreement;
– unilaterally by either party subject to applicable notice requirements; or
– in instances of gross misconduct as permitted under Article 44 of the Labour Law.

In addition to the above, the employment relationship will also be regarded as terminated in any of the following instances:

– Where the employer fails to perform its legal or contractual obligations, such as delaying payment of wages for more than sixty days.
– The employee is unable to attend work as the employer's place of work has been closed for more than two months and the employee has issued a complaint against the employer in this regard during such period which has subsequently been verified by an inspector from the MHRE.

– A court ruling in favour of the employee for unpaid wages of not less than two months' wages, arbitral dismissal or any other unpaid contractual or statutory sums without a legal justification.

Invalid Termination

Any termination exercised by either party will be considered invalid if any of the below circumstances can be shown:

– Where the above termination circumstances have not been followed.
– Where it is established that the employer employs a non-UAE national undertaking the same role as the terminated UAE national or where the termination has been processed in order to enable the employer to recruit a non-UAE national in place of the terminated UAE national.
– Termination is unrelated to the UAE national's employment or where the termination is as a result of the UAE national making a complaint to the MHRE against the employer which is subsequently proven true.

Enforcement and Penalties

Where it is established that the termination is invalid due to the reasons set out in the above section and the dispute is not settled amicably, the MHRE may undertake any of the following actions:

– refer the matter to the labour court;
– downgrade the employee's priority on the MHRE job-seeker register for a period of up to six months, thereby making it harder for the employee to find alternative employment using such register; and/or
– suspend the issuance of new work permits for the employer up to a period of six months.

The MHRE may also impose on employers a financial penalty of AED 20,000 per incident where any of the following is established:

– Breach of the decree or any of the guides issued following the publication of the decree.
– Illegal termination and failure to reinstate the employee to his or her role.
– Failing to make the appropriate pension contributions to the pension authority on behalf of the UAE national employee.
– Failing to adequately implement Emiratisation policies and requirements within the workplace where UAE nationals are employed.

24.2.   CHECKLIST OF DO'S AND DON'TS

– Monitor the employment of UAE nationals and their recruitment.
– Provide training and internship programmes as a means to recruit and locate suitable UAE candidates for recruitment.
– Establish relationships with organizations such as TANMIA, Young Arab Leaders, regulatory authorities, Chambers of Commerce, local educational institutions such as universities, in order to secure access to suitable candidates.
– Ensure compliance with the requirement to employ UAE nationals in reserved roles and through the Tawteen programme.
– Ensure any termination is in accordance with the Emiratisation Decree.

25.   RESOLUTION OF LABOUR, DISCRIMINATION AND EMPLOYMENT DISPUTES: LITIGATION, ARBITRATION, MEDIATION AND CONCILIATION

25.1.   INTERNAL DISPUTE RESOLUTION PROCESS

Employers should have grievance policies and procedures providing for the resolution of disputes or concerns internally and without resort to the MHRE or the free zone authority (as applicable).

25.2.   MEDIATION AND CONCILIATION

Employees or employers who are based onshore in the UAE and have complaints about employment practices (whether during the employment or on its termination) must go to the MHRE, which will try to resolve the dispute. Thereafter, any unresolved disputes may be referred to the Labour Court. For those sectors regulated by other government authorities, the Immigration Department has a complaints commission as an alternative to the MHRE's complaints section.

Employees or employers who are based within a free zone in the UAE must raise any complaints they may have with the relevant free zone authority. Thereafter, any unresolved disputes may be referred to the Labour Court.

Within the DIFC, most employment matters are initially directed to the Small Claims Tribunal which will attempt to conciliate the dispute, and which may then be referred to the DIFC Court depending on complexity and quantum. Within the ADGM, employment claims are to be heard by the

Court of First Instance and in particular either the Small Claims Division or the Employment Division.

In any dispute with an employee, whether before the MHRE or the courts in the UAE, the MHRE or the courts will look primarily at the MHRE Contract, which is taken to be the operative contract in the UAE. However, under Article 7 of the Labour Law, any supplementary contract is enforceable if its terms are more favourable to the employee.

25.3.   ARBITRATION

There is no legislative bar on arbitration, applying within an employment context. However, it may be that the MHRE will refuse to recognize an arbitration clause and hear a complaint in line with its authority to do so under Article 54 of the Labour Law. Furthermore, the Labour Court has in the past ruled that conciliation is not permissible in labour disputes, and therefore, arbitration is not permissible either. Therefore, even if the parties agreed to an arbitration clause in their contract, it is likely that the Labour Court would assume jurisdiction.

Arbitration is permitted in the DIFC and ADGM. A party wishing to invoke an arbitration clause must do so at the earliest opportunity in the dispute process and certainly at the earliest hearing and representations to the Court.

25.4.   LITIGATION

Litigation in the UAE involves a series of hearings at which each party submits written representations with supporting documents. A local advocate with rights of representation in the UAE courts can represent each party, although employees are not obliged to be represented and can represent themselves. Employees are also not subject to court fines or fees in order to raise claims arising out of their employment. The losing party does not usually bear the costs of the other party's legal fees but may be ordered to pay a nominal sum to the other party for its legal fees. Local advocates must have a specific power of attorney authorizing the advocate to represent and act for the employer in relation to the particular labour claim. This power of attorney must be registered with the court on the advocate's first appearance.

The time required for a claim to be heard is approximately three to six months for a decision at the Court of First Instance. Either party to the litigation may appeal this decision on either law or fact. The appeal process would take a further three to six months. A final appeal may be possible to the Court of Cassation.

25.5. FINES, PENALTIES AND DAMAGES

If an employer faces repeated complaints from employees at the MHRE, it is possible for the employer to be suspended from dealing with the Ministry on the basis that the employer has committed continuous violations of the Labour Law. Such a suspension could apply to all businesses registered under the authorized signatory's name.

Complaints could also trigger a labour inspection, and the MHRE can also impose a fine of between AED 5,000 and AED 1,000,000 for violation of the Labour Law and/or the Executive Regulations.

25.6. CHECKLIST OF DO'S AND DON'TS

- When faced with any MHRE complaint, a representative of the company should always attend.
- All relevant papers will need to be submitted in Arabic and translated by an official translator in order to be submitted for use in a Labour Court.

26. EMPLOYER RECORD-KEEPING, DATA PROTECTION, AND EMPLOYEE ACCESS TO PERSONNEL FILES AND RECORDS

26.1. OVERVIEW

An employer is under an obligation under the Labour Law, the DIFC Employment Law and the ADGM Employment Regulations to maintain certain records.

26.2. PERSONNEL FILES

The Labour Law requires employers to maintain general personnel files and maintain all records for a minimum of two years after the date of termination. Please refer to section 10.9 for more information.

The Labour Law is silent on the right of employees to have access to their personnel records or to ensure that their records are kept on file. However, the DPL provides employees or data subjects the right to request that their personal data are transferred to another controller, that inaccurate information is corrected, and the deletion of personal data in certain circumstances. The MHRE may also conduct labour inspections, at which point the employer may be required to rectify any failure to comply with their record-keeping obligations.

An employer must maintain personnel records detailing disciplinary action taken against an employee, the process followed, investigation completed and the sanction imposed. The employee has the right to have the imposed disciplinary sanction confirmed in writing.

Under the DIFC Employment Law, an employee must issue payslips to employees, maintain personnel records with all of the employee's information, and issue employees with written statements of their main terms and conditions of employment. These records should be maintained for six years.

As previously mentioned, the DIFC and ADGM data protection laws (please refer to section 22.1) prescribe rules and regulations regarding the collection, handling, disclosure and use of personal data in the DIFC and ADGM, the rights of individuals to whom the personal data relates and the power of the DIFC Authority and ADGM Board in performing its duties in respect of matters related to the processing of personal data as well as the administration and application of the relevant law. Such laws are applicable to personnel records.

26.3. CONFIDENTIALITY RULES

The Labour Law is silent on an employer's obligations with respect to employee privacy. However, the constitution guarantees the right to privacy, stating that 'freedom of communication by post, telegraph or other means of communication and the secrecy thereof shall be guaranteed in accordance with the law'.

The UAE Penal Code makes it an offence for a post (i.e., mail) to be opened by a person other than the stated recipient or addressee. It is also an offence to disclose another person's personal or confidential information without that person's consent.

With regard to the DIFC and ADGM, the DIFC Data Protection Law and ADGM Data Protection Regulations, respectively will apply, and an employer should maintain an employee's confidential information.

26.4. EMPLOYEE ACCESS

Under the DPL, DIFC data protection law and ADGM Data Protection Regulations, an employee is entitled to be given access to the information held by his employer.

There is no equivalent right under the Labour Law; however, an employee is entitled to certain documentation as being his or her personal property, such as a labour card and MHRE contract.

27. REQUIRED NOTICES AND POSTINGS

27.1. OVERVIEW

All employers must post written instructions regarding workplace safety measures that should be taken at the workplace.

Termination notices must be issued in writing.

27.2. CHECKLIST OF DO'S AND DON'TS

– All notices must be issued in writing.

9 789403 544441